ADDISON-WESLEY

QUEST 2000

EXPLORING MATHEMATICS

Randall I. Charles   David C. Brummett   Ricki Wortzman
Lalie Harcourt   Carne S. Barnett   Brendan Kelly

▼▼Addison-Wesley Publishing Company

Menlo Park, California • Reading, Massachusetts • New York
Don Mills, Ontario • Wokingham, England • Amsterdam • Bonn
Paris • Milan • Madrid • Sydney • Singapore • Tokyo
Seoul • Taipei • Mexico City • San Juan

The Professional Team

Contributing Authors

Elisabeth Javor, Los Angeles, California
Alma Ramirez, Oakland, California
Freddie Lee Renfro, Bay Town, Texas
Mary M. Soniat-Thompson, New Orleans, Louisiana

Multicultural Advisors

Barbara Fong, Atherton, California
Jeanette Haseyama, San Diego, California
James Hopkins, Seattle, Washington
Lyn Tejada Mora, San Diego, California
Glenna Yee, Oakland, California
Terry Walters, Encinitas, California
Roger E. W-B Olsen, San Francisco, California

Technology Advisors

Cynthia Dunham, Framingham, Massachusetts
Diana Nunnaley, Maynard, Massachusetts
Fred Crouse, Centreville, Nova Scotia
Flick Douglas, North York, Ontario
Susan Siedman, Toronto, Ontario
Evelyn Woldman, Framingham, Massachusetts

Editorial Coordination: McClanahan & Company

Design: McClanahan & Company

Cover Design: The Pushpin Group

ISBN: 0-201-84004-9

2 3 4 5 6 7 8 9 10 - VH - 99 98 97 96 95 94

Table of Contents

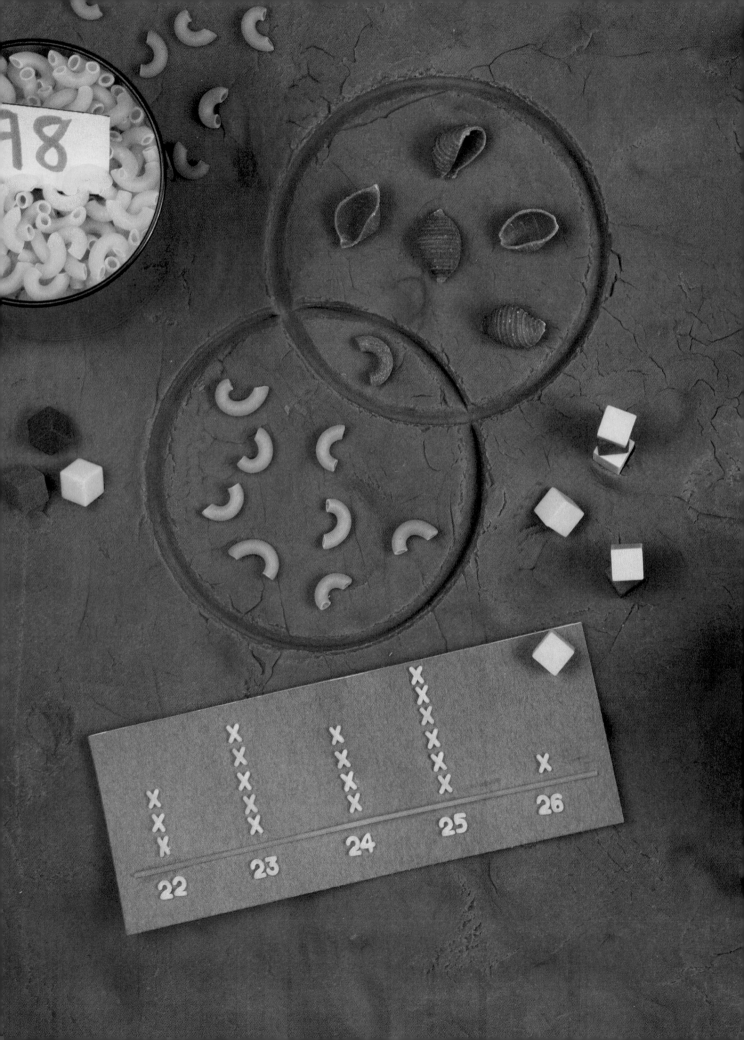

What patterns can we see in data?

Shoes, Shoes, Shoes!

▶ What data can you gather about shoes? Which data need numbers or measures? Which data can be described in other ways? What ways?

ON YOUR OWN

1. Talk with family members about the characteristics of shoes that are typical in your family. Below are some questions you might ask. Record your family's comments and answers.

   a. What are the characteristics of the most typical shoe you own? Explain.

   b. How can you describe the characteristics of a typical shoe for your family?

   c. What is the typical length of time that a shoe lasts in your family? How can you explain the variations?

   d. Are the characteristics of your favorite shoe typical of your other shoes?

2. Use the list of characteristics you made in problem 1 to draw a diagram like the one below. You can draw the shoes, cut pictures of shoes out of newspapers or magazines, or describe shoes in words.

3. *My Journal:* What does "typical" mean to you?

The Macaroni Plot

▶ A line plot can give us a quick picture of numerical data.
What numbers belong on the line plot?
What is the greatest number?
What is the least number?

Macaroni Graph

78   79 80 81 82 83 84 85 86

79

85

96

ON YOUR OWN

1. This line plot shows the number of times some fourth graders jumped rope. Write three statements based on the patterns you see in the data. What can you conclude about the jumpers?

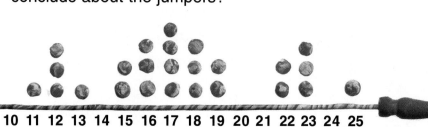

7 8 9 10 11 12 13 14 15 16 17 18 19 20 21 22 23 24 25

2. Michael bowls three games each week with his bowling club. His scores for five weeks are shown to the left. Show these scores on a line plot. Write five statements you can make about Michael's scores based on the line plot.

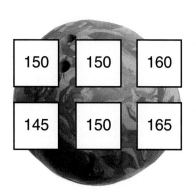

| 150 | 150 | 160 |
| 145 | 150 | 165 |

3. The line plot below shows ages of members of an after-school camera club. Suppose three new members joined the club and their ages were added to the plot line.

   a. Choose three ages to give a greater range for the data.

   b. Start with the original line plot. Give three ages you could add which would make the age that appears most an odd number.

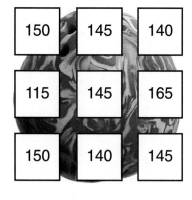

150	145	140
115	145	165
150	140	145

   c. Start with the original line plot. Give three ages you could add which would make the middlemost age be 14.

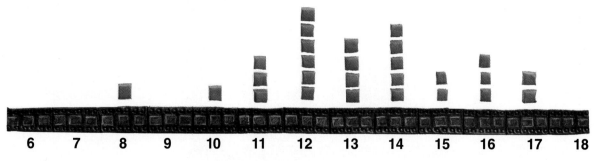

6   7   8   9   10   11   12   13   14   15   16   17   18

4. *My Journal:* What questions do you have about line plots?

Food for Thought

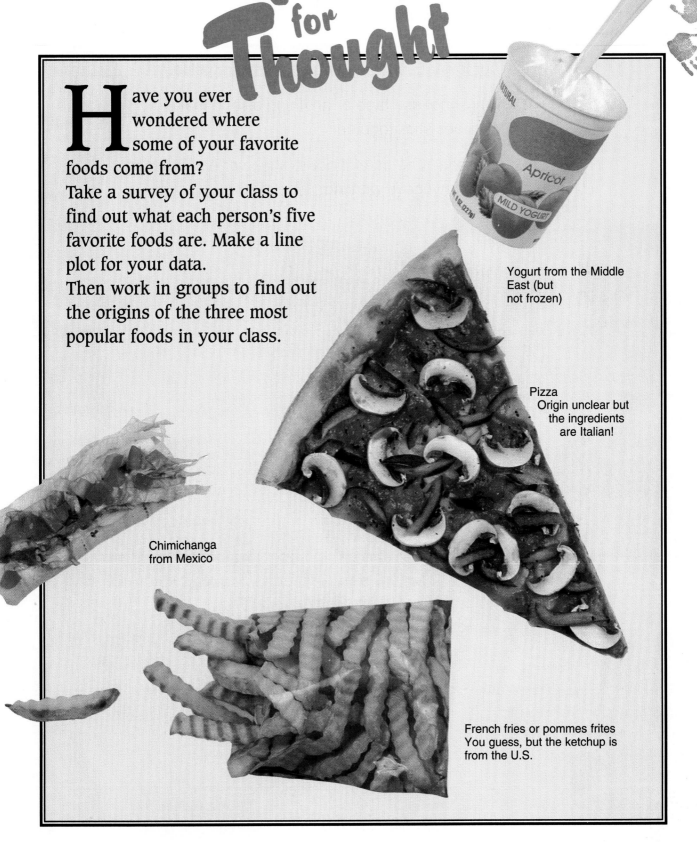

Have you ever wondered where some of your favorite foods come from?
Take a survey of your class to find out what each person's five favorite foods are. Make a line plot for your data.
Then work in groups to find out the origins of the three most popular foods in your class.

Yogurt from the Middle East (but not frozen)

Pizza
Origin unclear but the ingredients are Italian!

Chimichanga from Mexico

French fries or pommes frites
You guess, but the ketchup is from the U.S.

7

Toppling Towers

Directions for Building Towers

1. Use only 1 cube for your base.

2. Your tower cannot lean against anything else.

3. You cannot use tape or anything else to make the cubes stick together.

4. You need to be careful not to shake or bump tables where anyone is working.

Watts, California

Pisa, Italy

ON YOUR OWN

Here are data about twelve apartment buildings in one city neighborhood.

Building	Year Built	Stories	Apartments	Elevators	Entrances	Exterior
Carlton Arms	1947	10	50	2	2	brick
Kimball Court	1967	4	28	0	4	wood
Heritage Commons	1993	10	20	2	4	brick
The Parkview	1975	7	28	1	4	brick
Holmes House	1982	12	60	2	3	brick
Breezy Point	1959	3	12	0	2	wood
Greenberg Gardens	1970	3	15	0	3	wood
G.W. Carver Coops	1973	12	75	3	4	brick
Lincoln Towers	1990	15	150	5	5	brick
The Lakota	1896	10	20	2	5	brick
London Houses	1960	8	32	2	2	brick
San Remo	1925	10	20	2	2	brick

1. Make a separate line plot for each of the categories: number of stories, number of apartments, number of elevators, and number of entrances.

   Use your line plots and other data in the table to write a description of what a typical building in this neighborhood is like. Justify your conclusions using the line plot and data table.

2. Who would want to know the most typical characteristics of buildings in a neighborhood? How might they use these data?

3. *My Journal:* What have you learned about line plots?

Something Up Your Sleeve

Where should the measurement begin?
Where should it end?
How can you be sure that everyone
measures the same way?
What could you use if you don't have a
tape measure?

ON YOUR OWN

1. What is the typical hat size in your family? How can you find out? What data can you record? Try it! Write about what you did, what you found out, and what problems, if any, you faced.

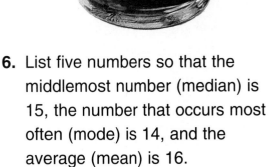

2. What is the average size of an egg? What measure(s) would you take? How many eggs would you examine to answer the question? Try it at home if you can. But be careful—don't drop any eggs as you investigate! If hardboiled eggs are available, use them.

3. Mindy read that the average goldfish lives for 6 years. Her goldfish is 6 years old. Should Mindy continue to buy fish food? Explain your thinking.

4. Kevin went to Dr. Hsia for his yearly check-up. Dr. Hsia said that Kevin was taller than average. What does this mean?

5. Lila likes to read. She reads a book of average length each week for the Library Club. This week she started a book of 435 pages which she knows she won't finish. What can she say about averages to convince the Library Club members that she is keeping up?

6. List five numbers so that the middlemost number (median) is 15, the number that occurs most often (mode) is 14, and the average (mean) is 16.

7. *My Journal:* What have you learned about means, medians and modes?

True or Not?

Typical Statements

- In 1991, a person in the United States spent about 70¢ on average to buy a dozen eggs.
- A working person saves on average 5¢ out of every dollar he or she earns.
- In the United States, a child (ages 6–11) watches on average $14\frac{1}{2}$ hours of television per week.
- An average writer uses on average about 20 words per sentence.
- An average adult man weighs 162 pounds.
- A person who leaves the water running while brushing his or her teeth wastes an average of about 6 gallons of water.
- A person in the United States uses an average of over 11 pounds of paper per week.

Create a statement like the ones to the left about the members of your class. Collect data on the statement, organize the data, and choose a graph to show your results. The data the class collects will help to describe what a "typical" student in your class is like!

CheckYOURSELF

Great job! Your data collection is complete and organized. You analyzed it and drew appropriate conclusions about the mean, the median, or the mode and communicated these clearly in writing.

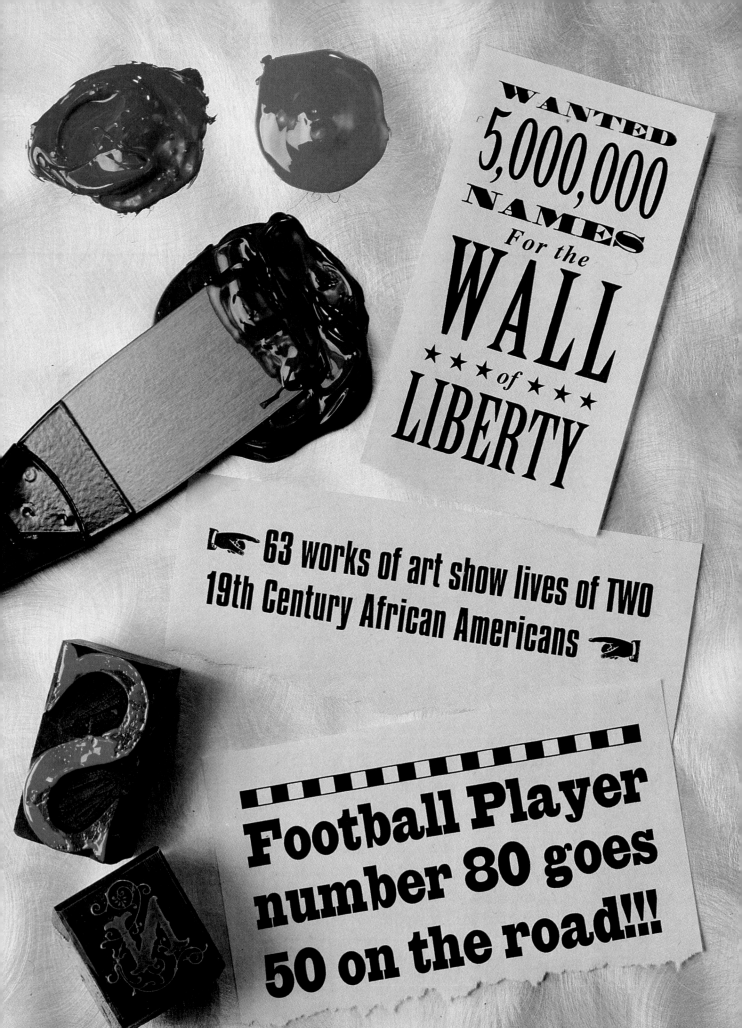

GRAND DISPLAY of 1,200 Poinsettias in SAN FRANCISCO

*H*ow can we show numbers?

TOONTOWN visitors enjoy 1,000,000 LAUGHS!

Lots of Blocks

▶ Estimate how many unit cubes in all.
Then find, write, and read the exact number.

1.

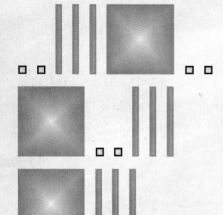

2.

3.

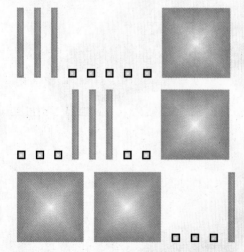

ON YOUR OWN

1. Write 4 numbers between 250 and 850. Draw base ten blocks to show each. Then write your numbers in words.

2. Write a number that is less than 700, greater than 600, and that has 0 tens. Draw base ten blocks to show your number. Then write your number in words.

3. How many multiples of 10 are there from 245 to 375? Remember, multiples of 10 end in 0.

4. How many times would the digit 5 be printed in writing the numbers 1 to 250? Prove your answer.

5. *My Journal:* What questions do you have about large numbers?

How Can You Decide?

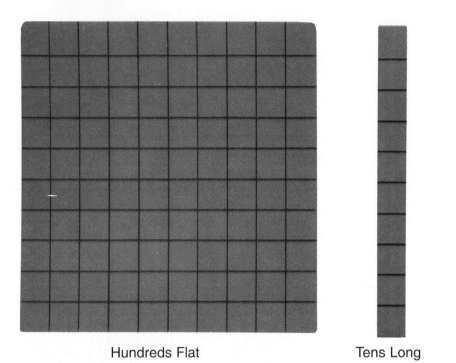

Hundreds Flat | Tens Long | Units Cube

What shape do you think a 1,000 block is?
What shape do you think a 10,000 block is?
What shape do you think a 100,000 block is?

To help you find out:

• Use base ten blocks.

• Try different arrangements of blocks.

• Draw pictures.

• Write to justify your conclusions.

• Compare your ideas with your classmates'.

• What did you discover?

ON YOUR OWN

1. Find examples of headlines or articles in the newspaper that show large numbers. Bring them to class to share.

2. Read the numbers aloud.

3. Write the numbers in words.

4. *My Journal:* What do you find difficult in working with large numbers? What do you find easy? Explain.

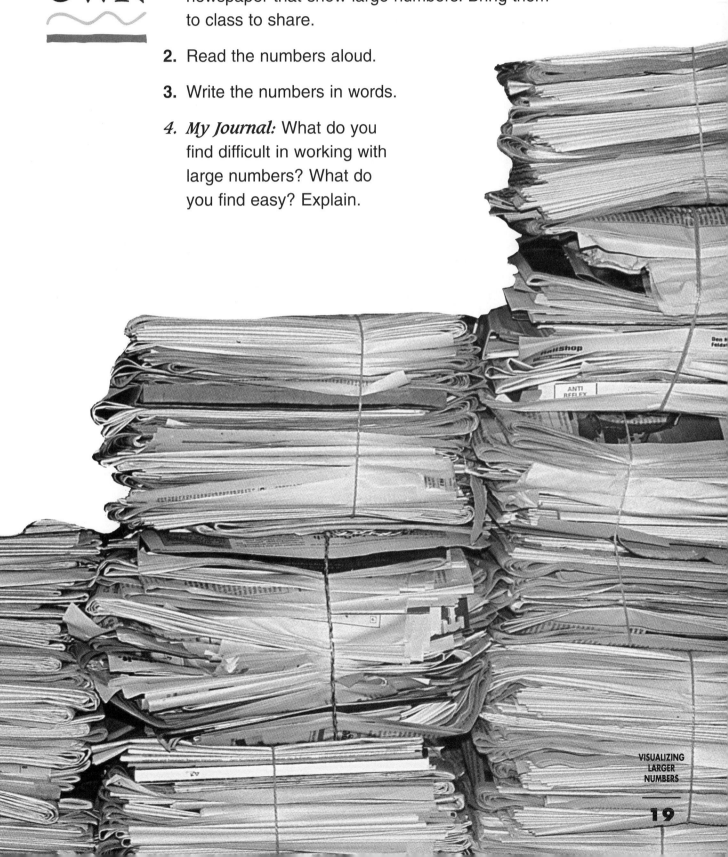

THE PLACE VALUE GAME

Group

2 players

Materials

Each player needs:

- a set of ten cards labeled 0, 1, 2, 3, 4, 5, 6, 7, 8, 9

- a set of six place value cards labeled ones, tens, hundreds, thousands, ten thousands, hundred thousands

Game Rules:

1 Each player arranges his/her place value cards in order in one row. Start with hundred thousands on the left and end with ones on the right.

2 Shuffle the two decks of number cards. Turn them face down.

3 Draw a card; higher number goes first.

4 The first player turns over one number card and places it above any of her/his place value cards.

5 The second player turns over one number card and places it above any of his/her place value cards.

6 The game continues until you both have filled your six place value positions with numbers.

7 Then compare the two numbers to find the greater number.

8 Whoever has the greater number wins!

ones

tens

hundreds

ten thousands

hundred thousands

6

2

6

hundred thousands

ten thousands

thousands

1 2 3 4 5 7 3 3

DIAL 6284 FOR MATH

H ave you ever wondered about ways other people used to represent numbers? Around 450 B.C.E. the people of Alexandria in northern Africa used a system of letters to represent numbers. The chart shows what some of the letters represented.

People today use letters for numbers. To make telephone numbers easier to remember many modern businesses choose 4- or 7-digit numbers that spell out appropriate words. The New York Knicks use 465-JUMP as their number.

A	represented	1
B	represented	2
E	represented	5
F	represented	6
H	represented	8
I	represented	10
K	represented	20
M	represented	40
N	represented	50
O	represented	70
P	represented	100
T	represented	300
X	represented	600

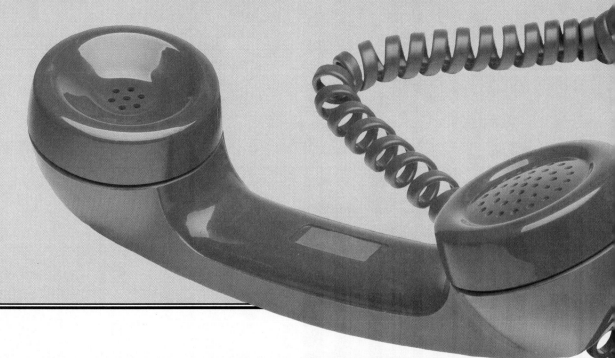

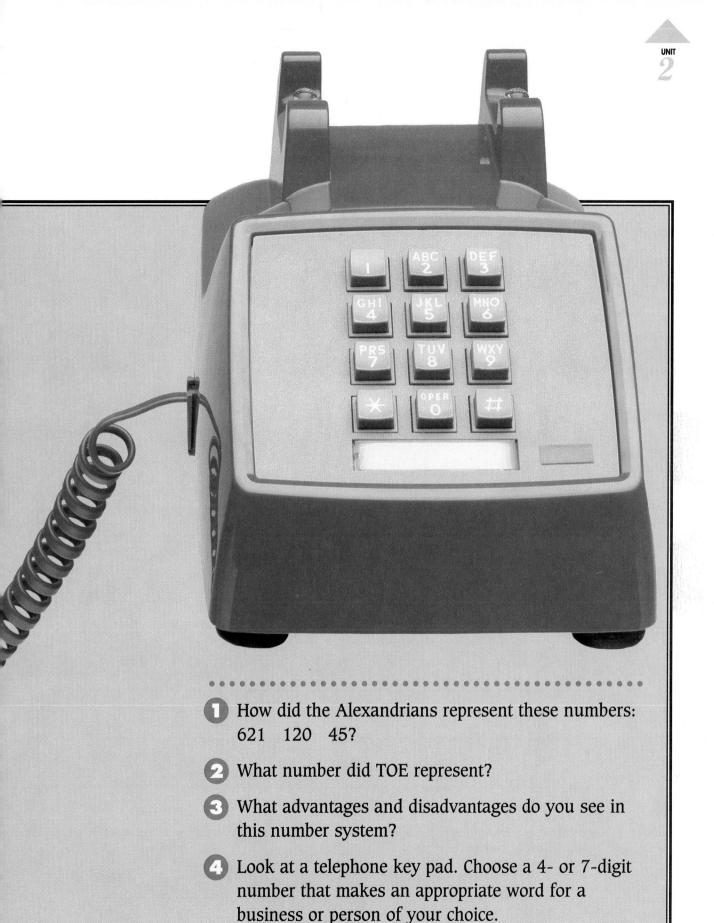

1. How did the Alexandrians represent these numbers: 621 120 45?

2. What number did TOE represent?

3. What advantages and disadvantages do you see in this number system?

4. Look at a telephone key pad. Choose a 4- or 7-digit number that makes an appropriate word for a business or person of your choice.

How Many Ways?

How many ways can you show 142 using hundreds, tens, and ones?

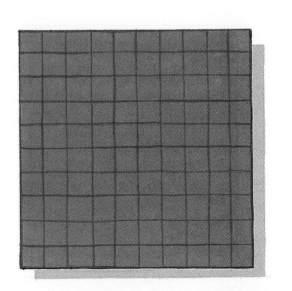  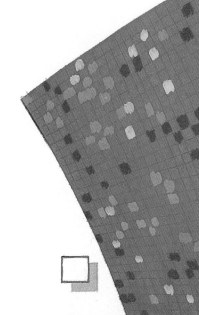

Hundreds	Tens	Ones
1	4	2
1	3	12

▶ Find as many ways as you can to show 142,000 using hundred thousands, ten thousands, and thousands.

Hundred Thousands	Ten Thousands	Thousands	Hundreds	Tens	Ones
1	4	2	0	0	0
1	3	12	0	0	0

Show for Everyone!

CORRECTIONS–GRADE 4 PAGE 26

▶ Read the descriptions of the TV shows to decide which ones would be of interest to different age groups.

Music of the Week
The top 10 CDs for the week are reviewed. Music groups often perform. (half-hour)

Adios!
A comedy about the daily activities of a Mexican American family living in Los Angeles, CA. (half-hour)

Plumber's Helper
A show specializing in helpful hints about fixing broken plumbing fixtures. (half-hour)

Boston Barristers
Interesting courtroom stories told from the plaintiff's and defendant's points of view. (1 hour)

Mysteries, Mysteries, Mysteries
A drama taking place in different locations showing detectives solving crimes. (1 hour)

The Warthogs
An animated show about a family of six living in New York. (half-hour)

Sea Diver
An hour-long adventure story starring two divers who specialize in locating and recovering lost treasures. (1 hour)

40/40

An in-depth analysis of four issues that are currently in the news. (1 hour)

What's New in Electronics?

An introduction to the newest electronic products available. (half-hour)

Room 14

A show about the funny and serious events occurring in a 4th grade classroom in Sacramento, CA. (1 hour)

Top Ten Television Shows					
	Audience				
Show	under 12	13–18	19–35	36–55	56+
Music of the Week	6,888,467	9,796,804	5,855,197	1,972,225	79,890
Adios!	7,934,685	8,760,512	5,663,243	4,896,432	888,776
Plumber's Helper	109,100	206,413	3,718,106	9,651,725	97,996
Boston Barristers	408,786	826,632	5,708,431	9,745,842	69,948
Sea Diver	2,504,634	5,754,973	7,598,542	8,633,906	3,899,542
40/40	393,531	1,442,786	4,978,506	9,865,040	2,999,542
What's New in Electronics?	4,988,957	8,758,947	9,857,046	7,623,486	534,807
Room 14	7,875,731	4,968,543	685,507	574,352	23,965
Mysteries	432,708	968,841	6,854,354	8,947,735	2,099,784
The Warthogs	9,846,009	8,947,846	6,463,957	4,896,534	65,863

Monday's Prime Time

7:00	7:30	8:00	8:30	9:00	9:30	10:00	10:30
News	Movies: Women from Michigan (92) ***					News	Let's Rap
Sports NBA Golden State at Cleveland				Movie: Parrot on my Shoulder ('92)			
Dayline	Planet Trek			Soul Train		Mysteries at Night	
Sports: Football Houston at New England				Movie: All About Adam ('92)			
Noticias	Movies: Dos Hombres ('94)**			Edicion Especial			Noticiero
Cantonese News		Korean News		Cantonese Drama		Tokyo News	

The Story Behind the Graph

▶ Look at the pictograph shown below and the bar graphs on the next page. What do they tell you?

▶ Choose one of the graphs. Use the information shown in that graph to help you write a newspaper article. Be sure that your article includes the large numbers shown in the graph.

1993 Major League Baseball Salaries

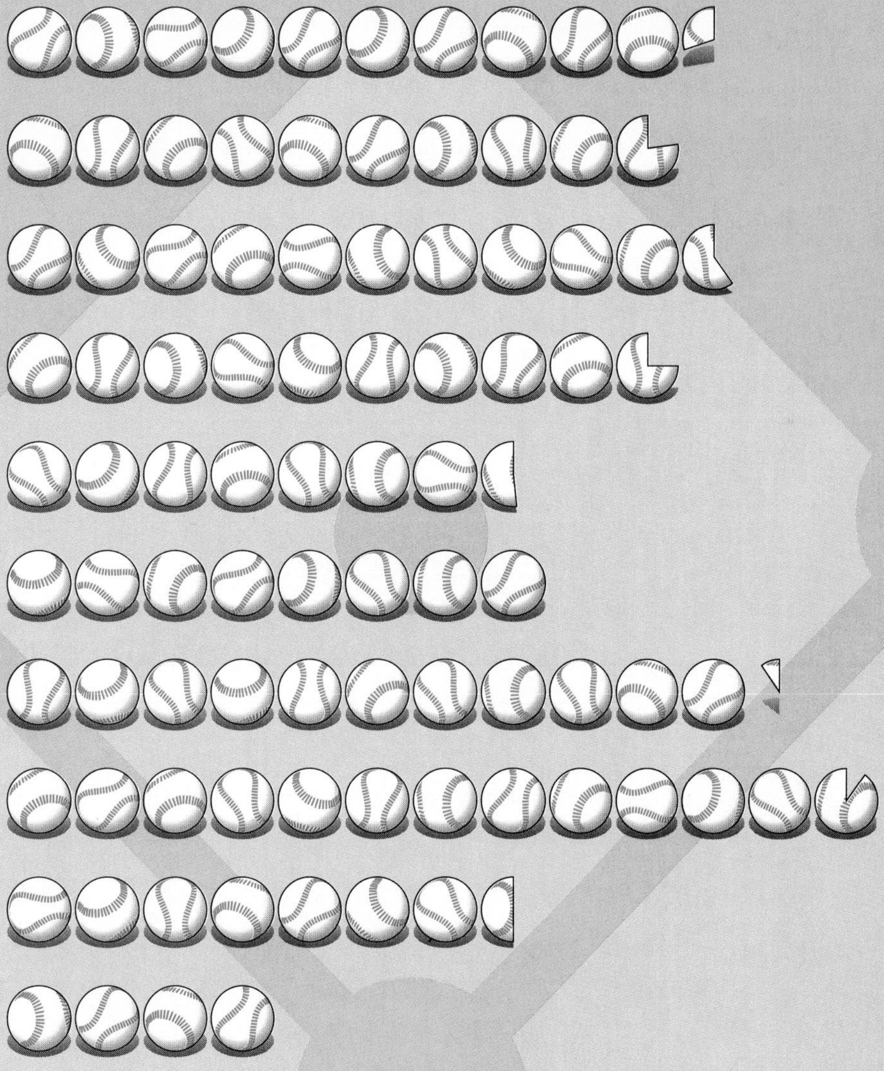

Player	Salary
Cal Ripken (Orioles)	$5,150,000
Roberto Alomar (Blue Jays)	$4,883,333
Kirby Puckett (Twins)	$5,300,000
Andre Dawson (Red Sox)	$4,875,000
Nolan Ryan (Rangers)	$3,757,000
Mark McGwire (Athletics)	$4,000,000
Danny Tartabull (Yankees)	$5,550,000
Bobby Bonilla (Mets)	$6,450,000
Kevin Mitchell (Reds)	$3,750,000
Mariano Duncan (Phillies)	$2,000,000

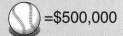 =$500,000

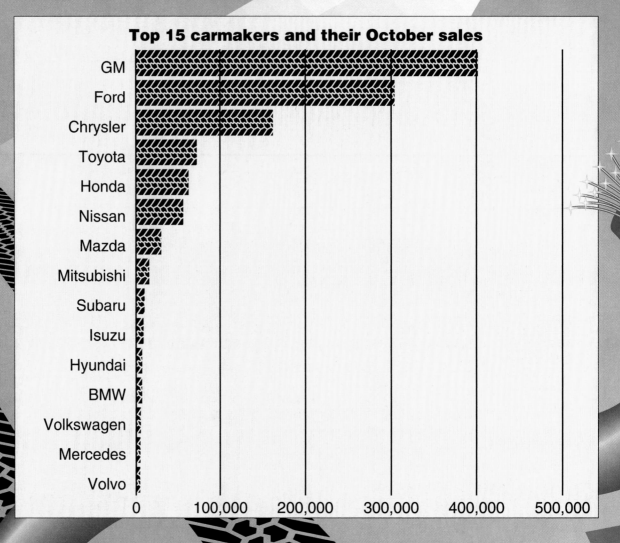

Top 15 carmakers and their October sales

GM
Ford
Chrysler
Toyota
Honda
Nissan
Mazda
Mitsubishi
Subaru
Isuzu
Hyundai
BMW
Volkswagen
Mercedes
Volvo

0   100,000   200,000   300,000   400,000   500,000

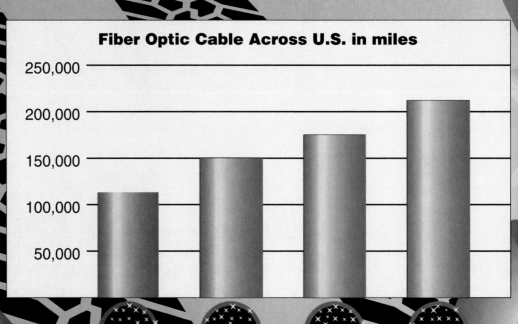

Fiber Optic Cable Across U.S. in miles

250,000

200,000

150,000

100,000

50,000

1989   1990   1991   1992

1. Think of a topic of interest to you about which you can use a graph to communicate information.

   Develop a plan and collect data that can be made into a bar graph.

Decide on a title and the labels you need.

Decide what numbers to use in the number scale.

When your graph is complete, write one addition and one subtraction question that can be answered from the information in your graph.

2. Make a bar or pictograph using the data below. Explain why you chose the graph you did.

3. *My Journal:* Do you prefer to show data with large numbers on a pictograph or bar graph? Explain your choice.

Air Distance in Miles						
	Atlanta	Boston	Chicago	Denver	Los Angeles	Montreal	New York
Atlanta		946	606	1208	1946	1046	760
Boston	946		867	1767	2611	254	187
Chicago	606	867		901	1745	742	740
Denver	1208	1767	901		849	1654	1638
Los Angeles	1946	2611	1745	849		2488	2475
Montreal	1046	254	742	1654	2488		333
New York	760	187	740	1638	2475	333	

USING
DATA
FROM A
GRAPH

BUILD A MODEL
1,000,000

What to do:

- Think about the cube-long-flat pattern used in base 10 blocks.

- What can you do to show 1 million cubes since you don't have 1 million of them?

- Work with the members of your group to decide on the shape and dimensions for your model of 1,000,000. Write and tell how you decided on the shape of your model cube and how you know it shows 1,000,000.

Materials
you might use:

- meter stick or metric
  measuring tape

- base 10 blocks

- centimeter grid paper

- scissors and masking tape

- tagboard or paper towel tubes

Discuss these questions with your group.

- Imagine you build a box that can hold a million 1-inch
  cubes. How many people about your size could fit
  inside the box?

- Would a million pairs of roller blades fit inside your
  classroom? a million bicycles?

- About how many marbles would fit inside a compact car?

CheckYOURSELF

Great job! Your millions model shows a clear
understanding of place value concepts. You communicated
your ideas well and showed clear thinking.

*H*ow can we describe shapes?

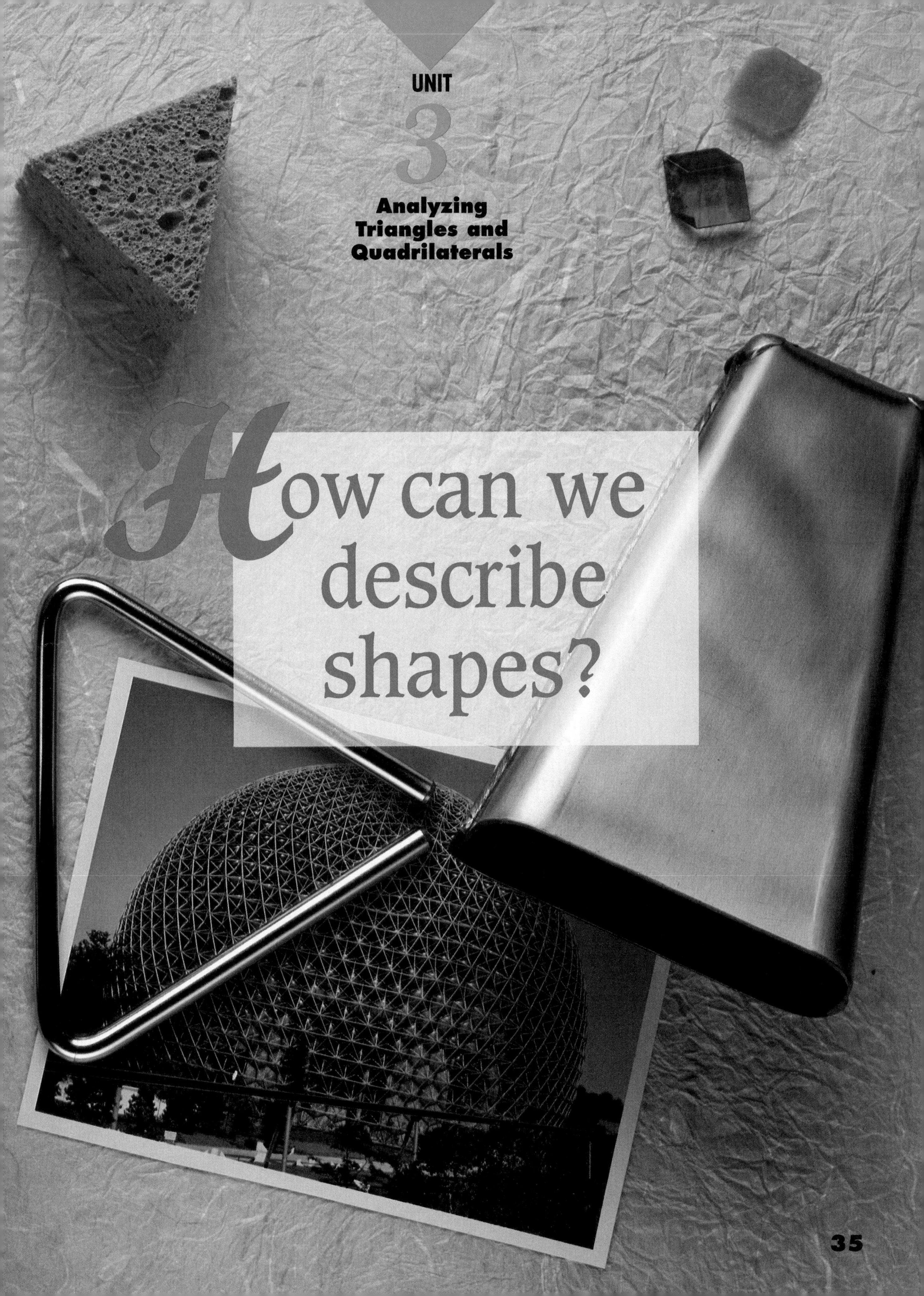

easure For Measure

▶ Use these guidelines to try
and make a triangle
with three pieces
of string.

 Cut a length of string.

 Decide where to make
the two cuts.

Cut the string in
three pieces.

Try to make a triangle with them.
Make sure the pieces are as
straight as possible. You may have
to fiddle a little with them. Make
sure the ends are touching.

Measure the pieces to the
nearest centimeter and record
the lengths in a chart.

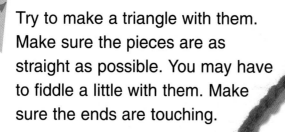

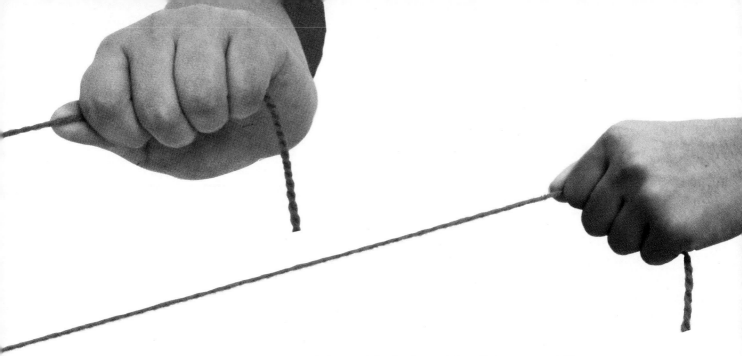

▶ Copy and extend the table below. Use it to record the lengths you cut. You may want to try other lengths.

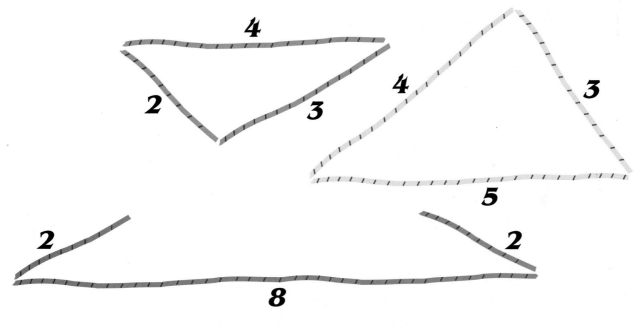

Sides			Longest Side	Other 2 Sides	Triangle?
1	2	3			
4	2	3	4	2, 3	yes
2	8	2	8	2, 2	no
5	3	4	5	3, 4	yes

EARLY SKYSCRAPERS

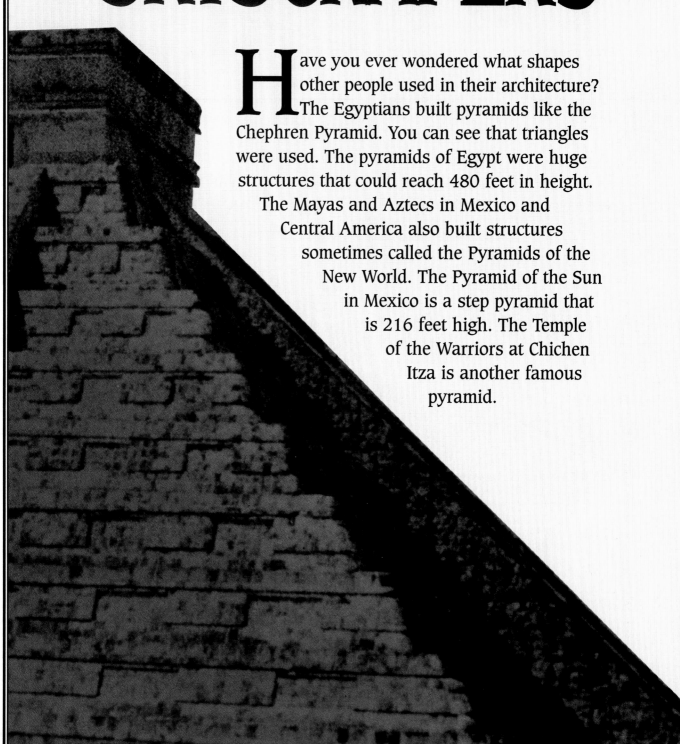

Have you ever wondered what shapes other people used in their architecture? The Egyptians built pyramids like the Chephren Pyramid. You can see that triangles were used. The pyramids of Egypt were huge structures that could reach 480 feet in height. The Mayas and Aztecs in Mexico and Central America also built structures sometimes called the Pyramids of the New World. The Pyramid of the Sun in Mexico is a step pyramid that is 216 feet high. The Temple of the Warriors at Chichen Itza is another famous pyramid.

Chephren Pyramid

Temple of the Warriors

Transamerica Building

1 What modern buildings have you seen or seen pictures of that are shaped like pyramids?

2 Describe the faces of the Chepren Pyramid. What shape do you think the bottom is?

3 How do the faces of the Mexican pyramids differ from triangular faces?

4 Construct a pyramid from paper. First decide how many faces you will need and what their shapes should be.

Triangles

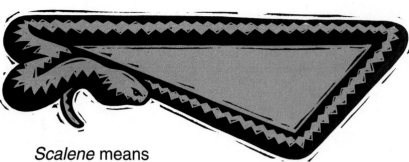

Scalene means "uneven" or "odd" and comes from a word meaning "serpent." No two sides of a scalene triangle are the same length.

Equilateral means "equal sides." All sides of an equilateral triangle are the same length.

Isosceles means "equal legs." Two sides of an isosceles triangle are the same length.

ON YOUR OWN

▶ Solve the problem.

1. Look for triangles at home and in your neighborhood. What kinds do you find? What are the different kinds of triangles used for? Copy and complete the chart to record your findings. Then write about what you found.

Type of Triangle	Use

2. *My Journal:* What have you learned about triangles so far?

The Most Beautiful Triangles

▶ How can you classify the triangles used in these stained glass windows?

ON YOUR OWN

▶ Solve the problems. Include drawings in your answers.

1. How could you group these letters by their angles?

A,E,F,H,I,K,L,M,N,T,V,W,X,Y,Z

2. Is it possible to have a right-scalene triangle? a right triangle which is not scalene? Draw pictures to illustrate your conclusion.

3. What is the most number of obtuse angles a triangle can have? acute angles? right angles? Write to justify your conclusions.

4. Maria claims that both triangles below are right triangles. Jon claims that only the one on the left is a right triangle. Whom do you agree with? Why?

5. *My Journal:* What did you learn that was new?

Divvy It Up

▶ Use your Power Polygons to make these shapes.
  Describe the characteristics. Include them on your chart.

Look at the quilt below.

1. How can you use rhombuses to make a bigger rhombus?

2. Which is the largest rhombus you can find in this design?

3. How many small rhombuses would you estimate there are in all?

4. What patterns do you see that could help you find all the rhombuses of different sizes?

5. *My Journal:* What did you find interesting about finding squares and rhombuses? Explain.

SECRET SHAPES

Pick one shape from the Polygons. Design a "hidden shape" puzzle of your own. Tell the puzzle solver what kind of shape to look for.

CheckYOURSELF

Great job! Your puzzle included a variety of hidden shapes in different sizes and/or positions. The puzzle was interesting for another student to solve—but not too hard! Your explanation of the answer was clear and complete.

World Records

The record number of table tennis hits in 60 seconds is 172.

The record number of somersaults performed on a trampoline is 75 in 1 minute.

The record number of hopscotch games played by one person in one day is 307.

The record set for bathtub racing is 90 miles in 24 hours.

The record number of footbag kicks in 5 minutes is 912.

The record speed for opening oysters is 100 in a little over 2 minutes.

The greatest distance covered by a team of leapfroggers is 999 miles in 10 days.

Hank Aaron holds the record for home runs: 755 during his 22-year career.

The furthest a basketball has been dribbled is 265 miles in 14 days.

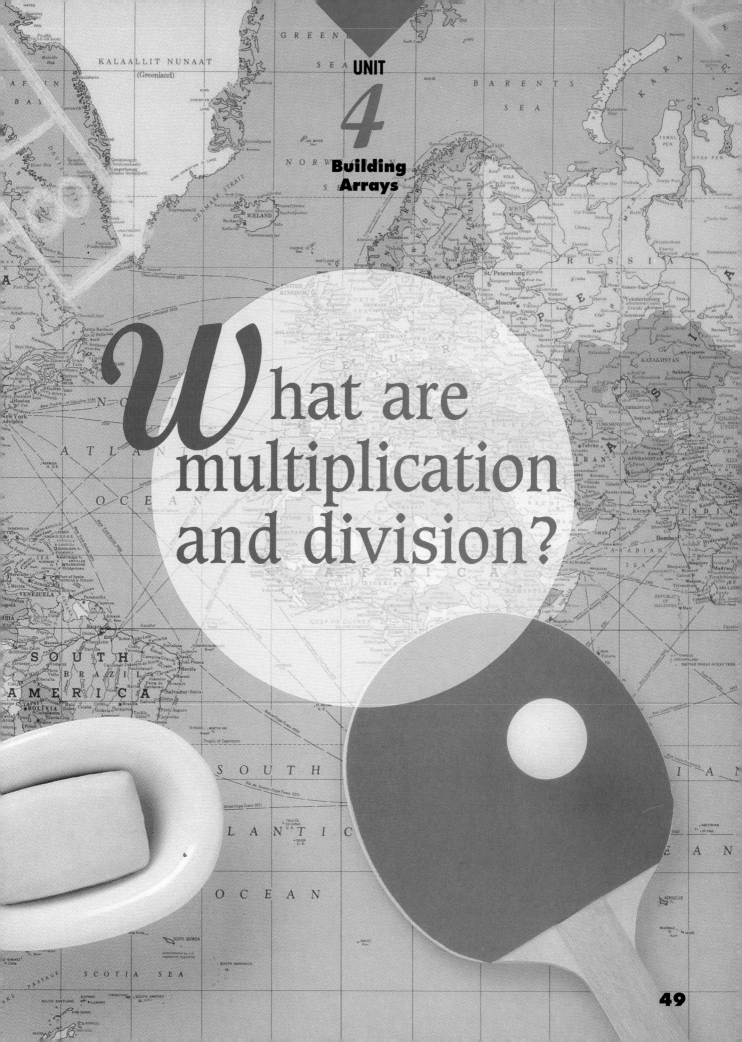

What are multiplication and division?

Rows, Columns, and Rectangles

Here are two ways to show the area of a 13 X 15 rectangle.

$$15$$
$$\times\ 13$$
$$100$$
$$30$$
$$50$$
$$15$$
$$195$$

$$13 \times 15 = 195$$

$$10 \times 15 = 150$$

$$3 \times 15 \rightarrow 3 \times 10 = 30$$
$$3 \times 5 = 15$$

$$150 + 30 + 15 = 195$$
$$13 \times 15 = 195$$

100

50

30

15

▶ Draw a picture of each rectangle using grid paper. Use your picture to find the area.

1. Find the area of the lawn.

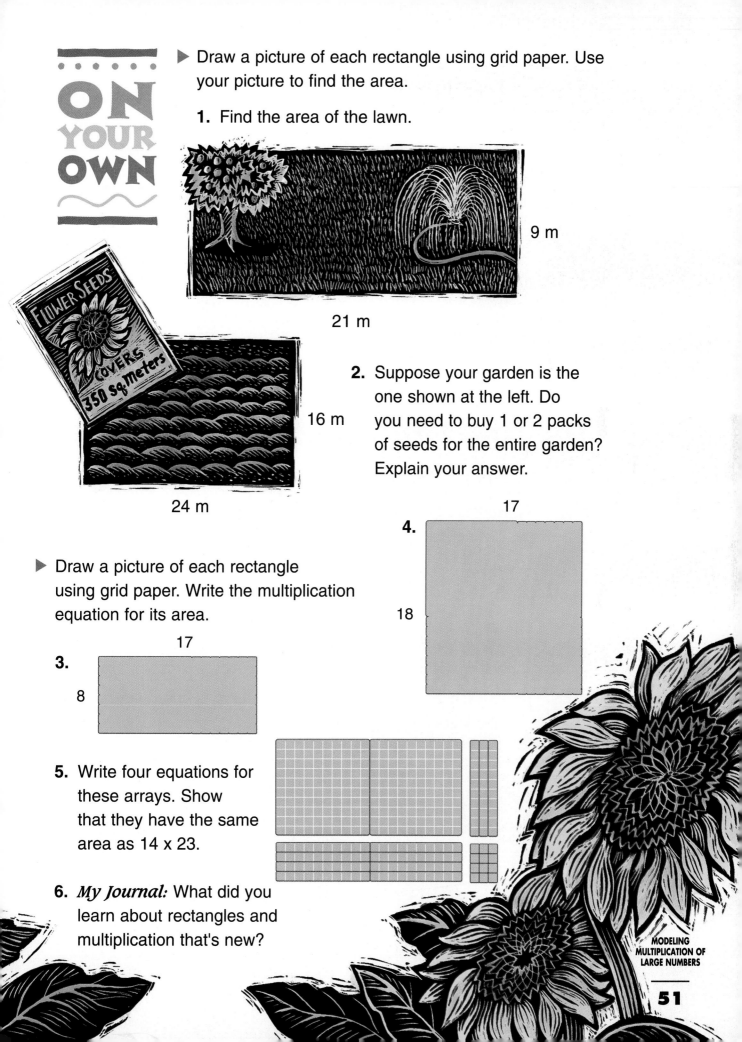

9 m

21 m

2. Suppose your garden is the one shown at the left. Do you need to buy 1 or 2 packs of seeds for the entire garden? Explain your answer.

FLOWER SEEDS
COVERS
350 sq meters

16 m

24 m

▶ Draw a picture of each rectangle using grid paper. Write the multiplication equation for its area.

17

3.

8

17

4.

18

5. Write four equations for these arrays. Show that they have the same area as 14 x 23.

6. *My Journal:* What did you learn about rectangles and multiplication that's new?

Different ... Yet the Same

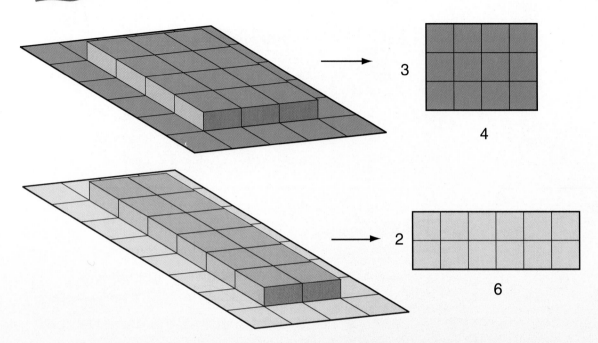

3

4

2

6

1. How are the two rectangles alike?

2. How are the two rectangles different?

ON YOUR OWN

▶ Determine whether each number is a prime number or a composite number. Draw at least two different rectangles on grid paper for each number that is composite.

1. 20   **2.** 18   **3.** 19

4. 9   **5.** 37   **6.** 21

▶ Marcos is planning to build a rectangular pen for his dog that has an area of 72 square feet. Each side will be a whole number of feet.

7. Draw on the grid paper the different pens he could build.

8. If you were Marcos, which pen(s) would you build? Why?

9. If you were Marcos, which pen(s) wouldn't you build? Why?

10. *My Journal:* What did you learn from this activity that you didn't know before?

Caught in the Middle Again

Is it in the range?

$$24 \times \underline{\ ?\ } \quad \text{Range:} \quad \genfrac{}{}{0pt}{}{950}{850}$$

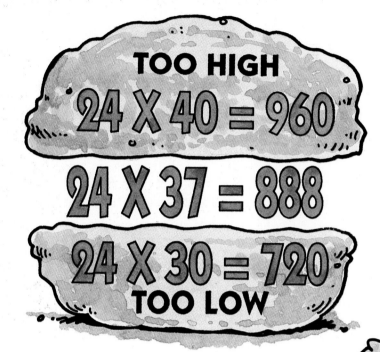

TOO HIGH

24 X 40 = 960

24 X 37 = 888

24 X 30 = 720

TOO LOW

▶ Use estimation to find the missing factor so the product is in the given range.

1. $18 \times \underline{\ ?\ }$ Range: $\genfrac{}{}{0pt}{}{300}{250}$

4. $98 \times \underline{\ ?\ }$ Range: $\genfrac{}{}{0pt}{}{7000}{5000}$

2. $72 \times \underline{\ ?\ }$ Range: $\genfrac{}{}{0pt}{}{500}{400}$

5. $52 \times \underline{\ ?\ }$ Range: $\genfrac{}{}{0pt}{}{4500}{3500}$

3. $27 \times \underline{\ ?\ }$ Range: $\genfrac{}{}{0pt}{}{200}{600}$

6. $45 \times \underline{\ ?\ }$ Range: $\genfrac{}{}{0pt}{}{3500}{3000}$

ON YOUR OWN

▶ Use estimation to find a range in which the exact answer lies. Show how you found your range.

1. 18 X 42   **2.** 67 X 35   **3.** 92 X 51

4. Write a multiplication expression whose product is in the given range:

a. ? X ?   Range: 500 / 400

b. ? X ?   Range: 1,750 / 1,200

5. Use estimation to give a range for the total number of sandwiches you might eat from now until you are 21 years old. Explain how you made your estimate.

6. *My Journal:* What are some things you know about estimation?

Have It Your Way!

▶ Estimate each product. Then find the exact answer. Compare your answer to your estimate. Be prepared to explain the strategies and procedures you used.

Chalkboard Talk!

1. 37 × 9   3. Fifty-eight times forty-six

2. 62
   ×13

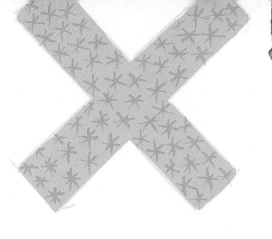

ON YOUR OWN

▶ Copy the boxes and write the digits in each.

1. Use the digits 2, 3, 4, and 5 to make the largest product possible.

×

2. Use the digits 2, 4, 6, and 8 to make the smallest product possible.

3. Explain if your answers to problems 1 and 2 would have changed if you could have multiplied a 3-digit by 1-digit number.

4. Use the digits 1, 2, 3, and 4 to make two factors whose product is even.

5. Use the digits 1, 2, 3, and 4 to make two factors whose product is odd.

6. *My Journal:* Which strategies or procedures for doing multiplication do you find most useful? Explain.

**MULTIPLYING
LARGE NUMBERS**

Inside and Out

Rules for inside and out.

1 Find the product of the outer numbers.

2 Find the product of the inner numbers.

3 Record the outer and inner products.

4 Repeat this two more times using different groups of consecutive whole numbers.

5 Write and describe a pattern you see in the products.

Pattern One

Use 4 consecutive whole numbers.

12, 13, 14, 15

inner numbers
outer numbers

13x14=182

12x15=180

Pattern Two

Use 4 consecutive even numbers.

12, 14, 16, 18

inner numbers
outer numbers

14x16=224

12x18=216

Pattern Three

Use 4 consecutive odd numbers.

11, 13, 15, 17

inner numbers
outer numbers

13x15=195

11x17=187

Aladdin's Arrays

Did you ever wonder why arrays make good models for multiplication? Advertisements often refer to a typical rug as 9 by 12. What they mean is the rug's length is 12 feet and its width is 9 feet. If you draw a picture of the rug on grid paper you can easily find the area of the rug.

1 Another popular rug size is 6 feet by 9 feet. Draw an array on grid paper to find its area.

2 A large rug is 12 feet by 18 feet. Draw an array on grid paper for it and find the area.

3 Some of the most beautiful oriental rugs, although rectangular, have somewhat unusual sizes. How would you find the area of an oriental rug that measures 6 feet 3 inches by 8 feet 6 inches? Draw a diagram on grid paper.

4 What patterns do you see in these rugs?

5 Make a drawing of a rug you like on grid paper. Label its length and width, then find its area. Add any designs you like.

Catch It—Quick!

▶ Follow these steps to measure your reaction time.

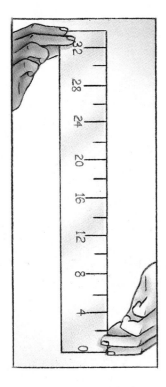 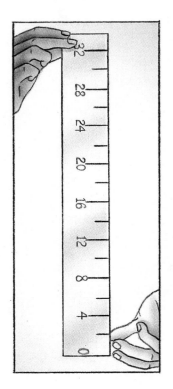

1 Hold a centimeter ruler upright near the 0 centimeter mark at the bottom. Have your partner hold the ruler near the top and record the holding point to the nearest centimeter.

2 Release the ruler from the bottom keeping your fingers about 1 centimeter from the ruler.

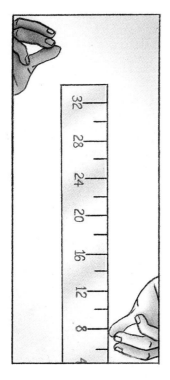

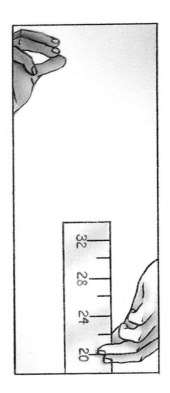

3 Have your partner release the ruler from the top.

4 Catch the ruler with your fingers as quickly as you can. Record the position your fingers are at to the nearest centimeter.

Find the difference between the starting mark and the ending mark—this is the reaction time. For example, if you follow the illustrations the reaction time is: 20 − 0 = 20.

Repeat this two more times for each person. Then find the average reaction time.

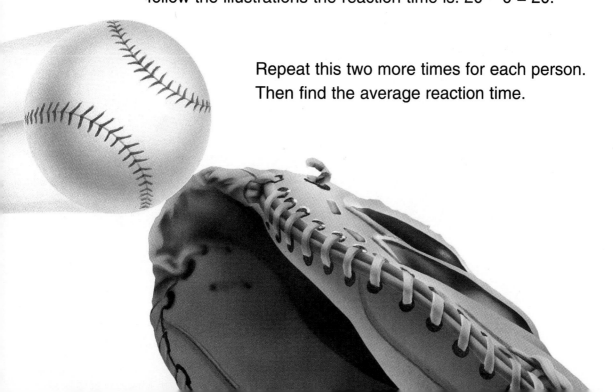

A Room Full of Dollars

▶ About how many dollar bills are needed to fill your classroom?

Here's some information to help you get started.

A dollar bill is about 6.5 cm wide and 15.5 cm long.

About 6 dollar bills cover one sheet of typing paper.

Mystery Rectangles

▶ Use base ten blocks to determine what each complete rectangle looks like. Then write a multiplication equation for its area. Tell if there are any blocks left over.

1. 162 square units

9 columns

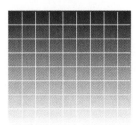

2. 230 square units

7 rows

3. 223 square units

12 rows

4. 408 square units

24 rows

5. 425 square units

15 columns

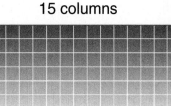

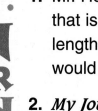

1. Mr. Hernandez is planning to build a patio that is 240 square feet. Name possible lengths and widths he could build it. Which would be the best length and width? Why?

2. *My Journal:* Explain how multiplication and division are related. Use examples.

MODELING
DIVISION OF
LARGE NUMBERS

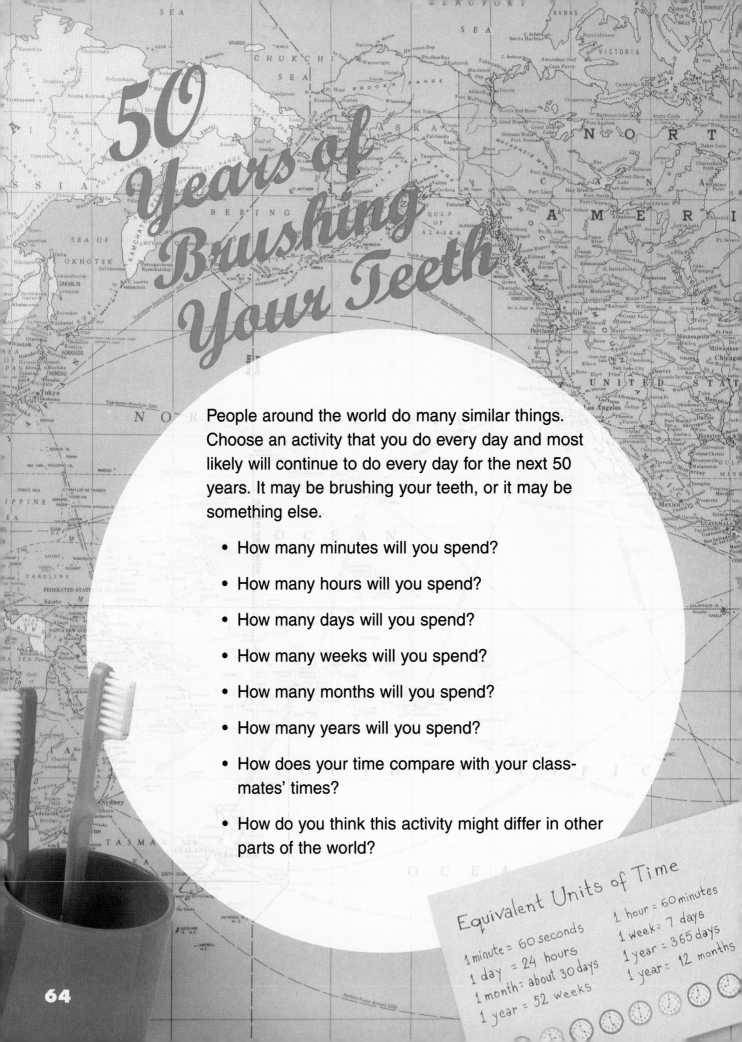

50 Years of Brushing Your Teeth

People around the world do many similar things. Choose an activity that you do every day and most likely will continue to do every day for the next 50 years. It may be brushing your teeth, or it may be something else.

- How many minutes will you spend?

- How many hours will you spend?

- How many days will you spend?

- How many weeks will you spend?

- How many months will you spend?

- How many years will you spend?

- How does your time compare with your classmates' times?

- How do you think this activity might differ in other parts of the world?

Equivalent Units of Time

1 minute = 60 seconds
1 day = 24 hours
1 month = about 30 days
1 year = 52 weeks

1 hour = 60 minutes
1 week = 7 days
1 year = 365 days
1 year = 12 months

Check YOURSELF

Great job! You used multiplication to find how much time you would spend in 50 years. Then you used multiplication and division appropriately to change that amount of time into other units of time. You wrote clearly about your work.

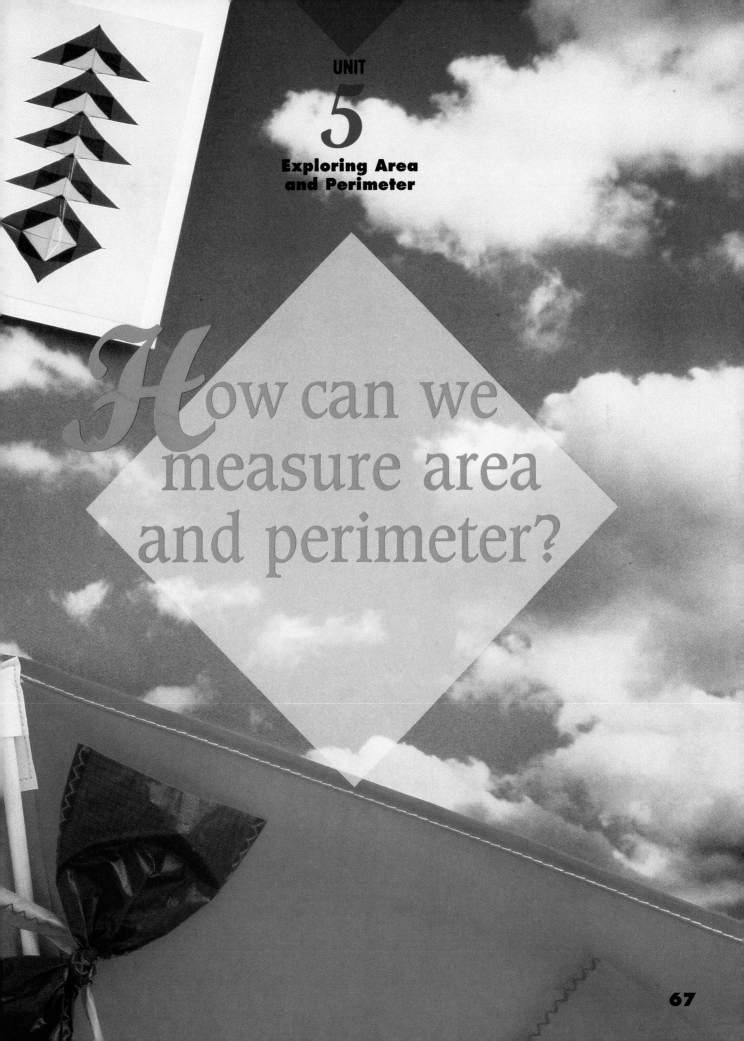

*H*ow can we
measure area
and perimeter?

Is It Allowed?

▶ Notice the edges of each block.
Designs like these are ALLOWED.

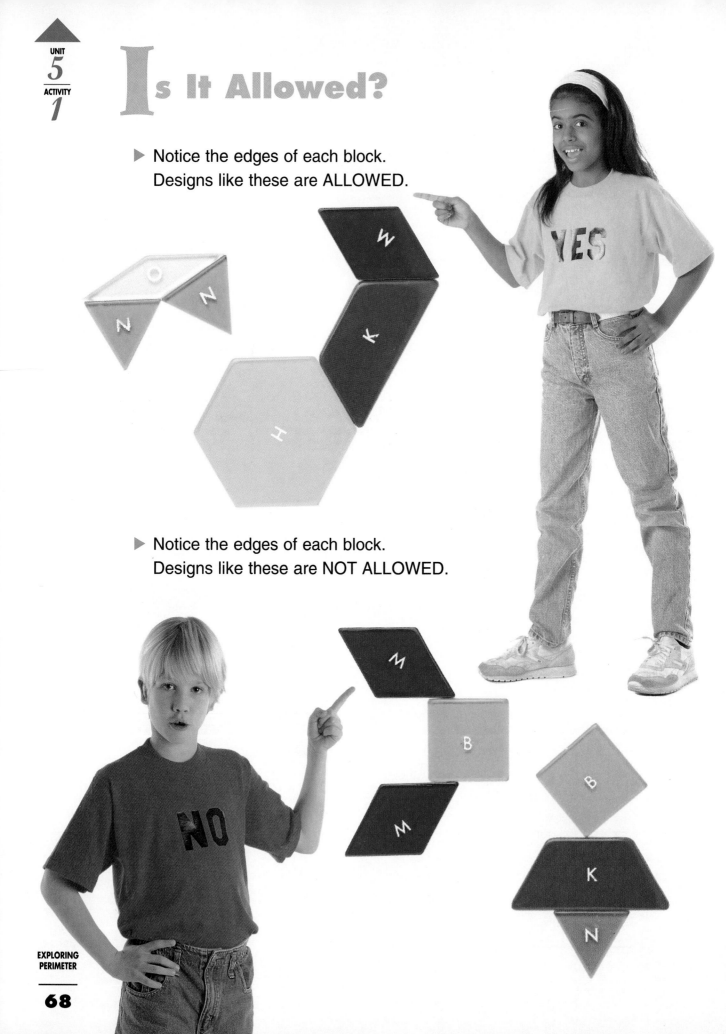

▶ Notice the edges of each block.
Designs like these are NOT ALLOWED.

Cutting Up

▶ Cut a rectangle into 4 different *polygons*—pieces with straight sides.

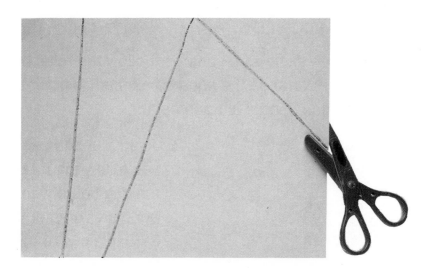

▶ Rearrange the pieces into a new figure.

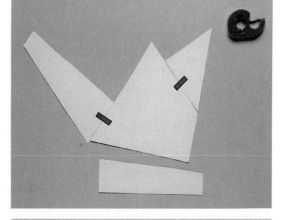

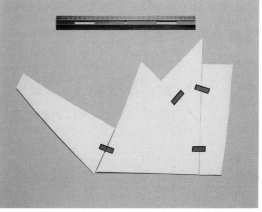

▶ Find the perimeter.
Remember, *perimeter* is the distance <u>around</u> the shape.

DIFFERENT
PERIMETERS,
SAME AREA

69

ON YOUR OWN

ALLOWED   **NOT ALLOWED**

1. Use three same-size squares. Follow the rule shown above. Rearrange the squares as many different ways as you can. Find each perimeter.

2. Using four squares, can you follow the rule and make a figure with a perimeter greater than 8? Explain your thinking. Draw pictures to show your solutions. The perimeter of the figure shown is 8 units. Its area is 4 square units.

3. How many arrangements of four squares have a perimeter of exactly 10 units?
   Draw these arrangements.

4. Find the 4-square figures with the least and the greatest perimeters. What can you say about them?

5. Do you always increase the perimeter when you cut a figure into more pieces?

6. When you cut a piece of paper into pieces do you ever change the area?

7. *My Journal:* What did you learn that is new in this activity?

The Puzzling Pooch Pen

You have 24 feet of fencing. You want to build a rectangular pen for your dog. What is the greatest area you can enclose with that much fencing?

AMAZING
F A C T S

Australia has the world's longest fence. It is made of wire and designed to keep out dingoes, wild dogs that can attack sheep. This fence is 3,437 miles long. That's about the distance from Vancouver, British Columbia, Canada, to Miami, Florida!

ON YOUR OWN

perimeter = 40 cm

6 cm

1. What is the length of this rectangle?
   Tell how you know.

2. Lyle baked a birthday cake for his dog. The cake was a rectangle 30 centimeters long and 20 centimeters wide. Lyle put a candle every 5 centimeters around the edges of the cake. How many candles did he use? Draw a picture on grid paper to show your solution.

3. The blue card covers part of the green shape. All sides of the green shape have the same length. The perimeter of the green shape is 48 centimeters. How many sides does the green shape have? Draw how you think it looks.

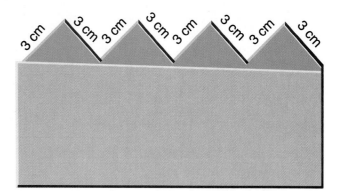

3 cm 3 cm 3 cm 3 cm 3 cm 3 cm 3 cm 3 cm

4. Draw a 5-sided figure that has a perimeter of 32 centimeters.

5. *My Journal:* What did you discover about the area you can enclose with a given length of fencing if the area must be rectangular?

In the Area

A.

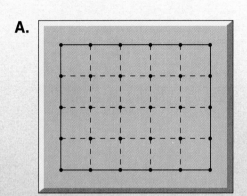

▶ Area = 20 square units

B.

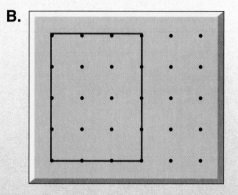

▶ Area = 12 square units

AREAS OF
RECTANGLES AND
TRIANGLES

Gee, Geoboards!

▶ What is the area of each figure?
How can you figure it out?

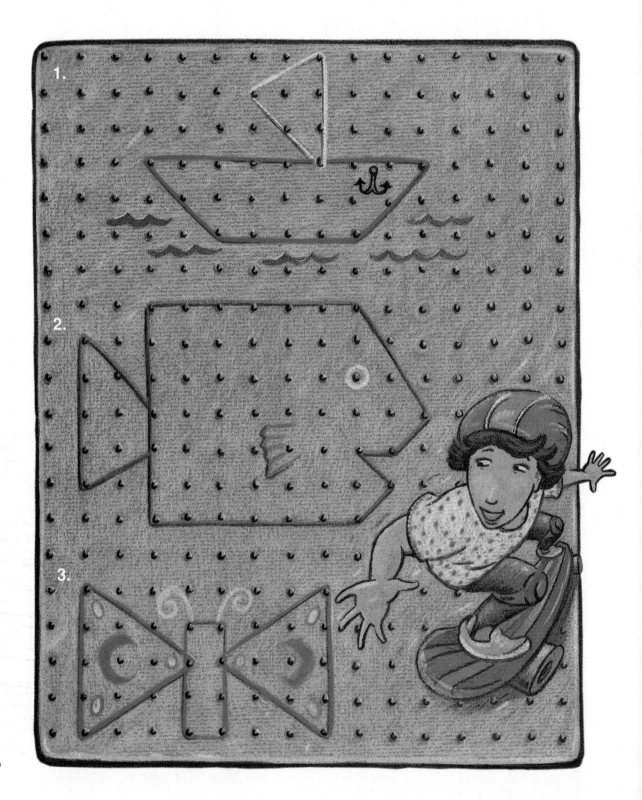

ON YOUR OWN

▶ Find the area of each figure.

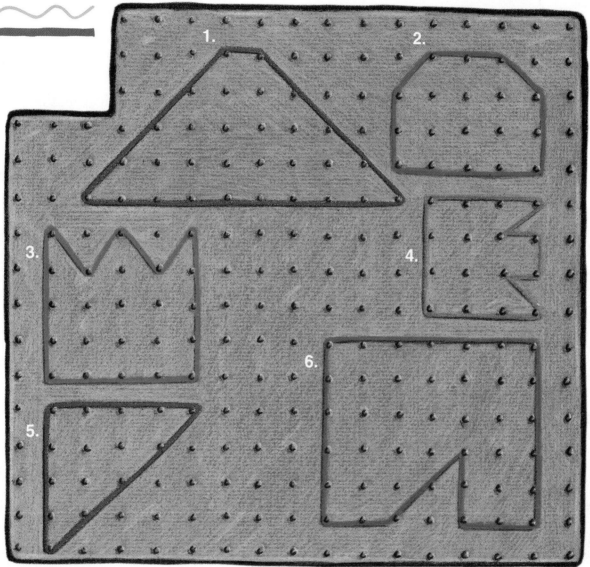

7. Get a piece of dot paper. Make any shape on it you like, as long as it has straight sides. Find the area of your shape. Be prepared to explain how you did it.

8. *My Journal:* Which problem on this page was easiest? Explain why.

Long or Tall

Houses

The longhouse was a rectangular, barrel-rooted house. The Iroquois Indians called themselves the *Haudenosaunee,* meaning "People of the Longhouse."

The Iroquois people of North America frequently built homes that many families shared. These homes were called longhouses. Each family had some private space, but hallways and fireplaces were shared.

The table at the right shows some typical dimensions of longhouses.

Length (in feet)	Width (in feet)
50	16
75	18
100	20
150	22

Have you ever wondered how people decide on the sizes of their homes? One of the factors that is considered is the number of people that are going to live there.

1 Find the area and perimeter of each longhouse. Which would you expect to be used by the largest number of families? If the smallest longhouse held 2 families, how many would you expect the largest to hold?

2 Today's apartment building or "tall houses" have private areas for families and some shared areas. Tell how you think these buildings are like longhouses and how they differ.

3 What private areas does your class have at school? What school areas are shared? Find the dimensions, area, and perimeter of some of these. Explain why you think they are the size they are.

4 Design a home or room with dimensions you like. Find its area and perimeter. Explain why you chose the size you did.

Right Triangle Search

How many right triangles with different areas can you make on your geoboard?

1. What is the area of each triangle?

a.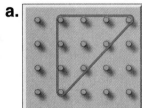

b.

c.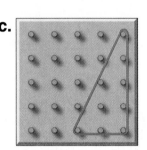

2. Which of the following shapes has an area of 2 square units?

a.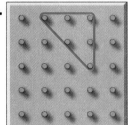

b.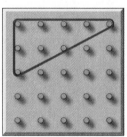

c.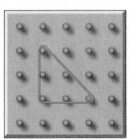

3. Which of these do *not* have an area of 1.5 square units?

a.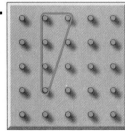

b.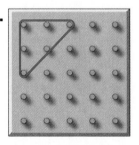

c.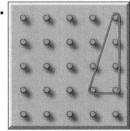

Irregular Shapes—Dot's Nice

1.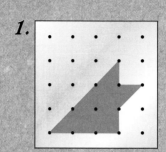

2.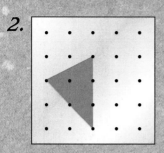

3.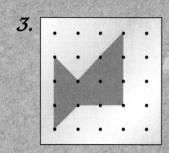

4.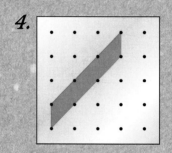

5.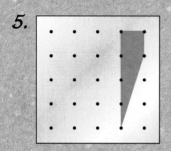

6.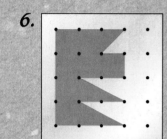

7.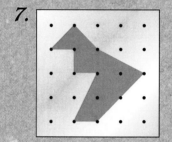

8.

9.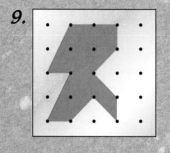

AREA OF
IRREGULAR
FIGURES

Go Fly a KITE

Design A Kite

Points to Remember:

- Design the kite.

- Plan its shape.

- Find its size.

- Figure the perimeter.

- Figure the area.

- Write clear directions.

- Check your work.

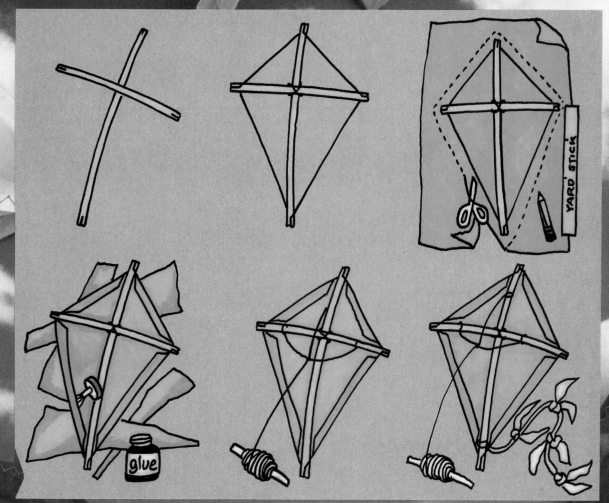

CheckYOURSELF

Great job! Your kite design and instructions show that you understand the concepts of perimeter and area. Your kite is interesting and attractive and looks like it will fly. You wrote step-by-step instructions with illustrations that communicate clearly the way to make your kite. You wrote about your use of perimeter and area in your description of your kite's size.

UNIT

6

Exploring Fractional Parts

How can we show and use fractions?

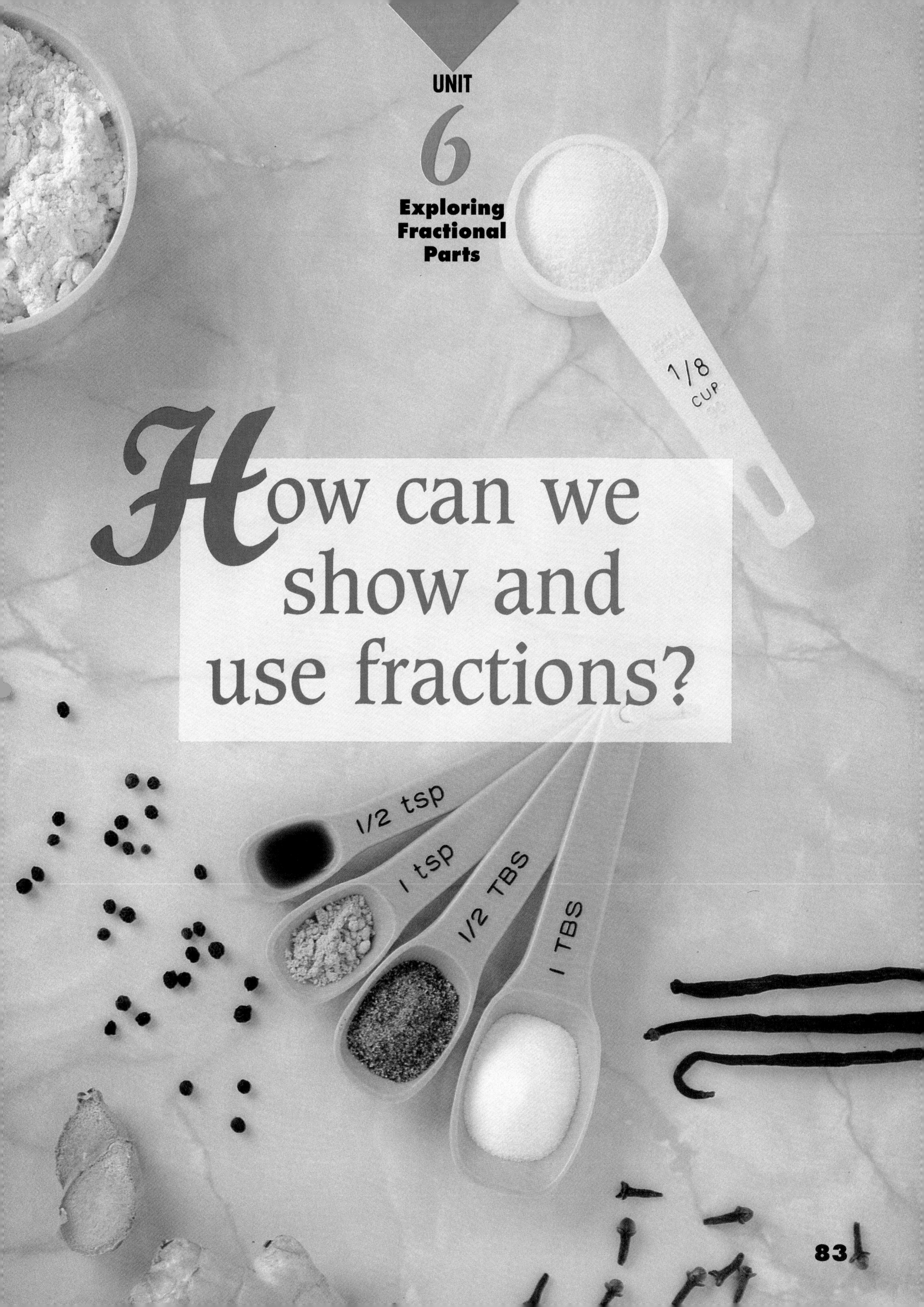

1/8 CUP
1/2 tsp
1 tsp
1/2 TBS
1 TBS

Can I Halve That?

▶ What is the area of each part?

Can I have the bigger half?

Picture That Fraction

▶ What is the area of each part?

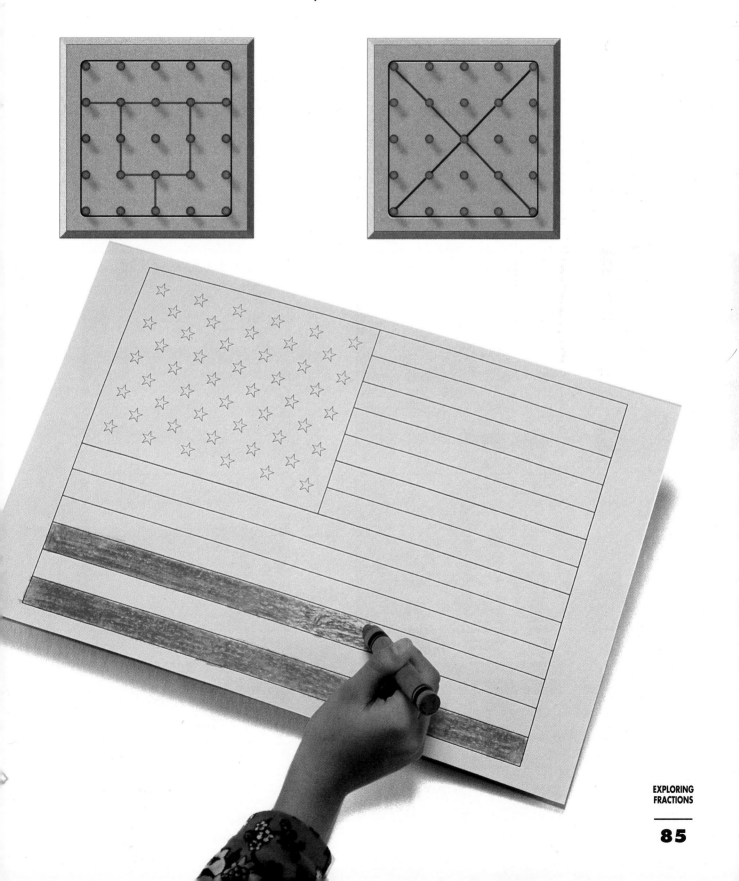

ON YOUR OWN

▶ Estimate the fractional part of the whole each color section is on each flag.

▶ Name the section by its color and write the fraction.

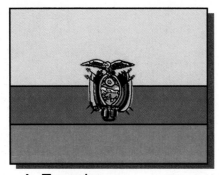

1. Ecuador

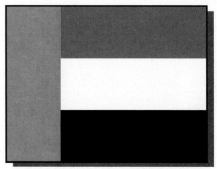

2. United Arab Emirates

3. Madagascar

4. Spain

5. Canada

6. Thailand

7. Suriname

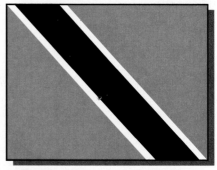

8. Trinidad and Tobago

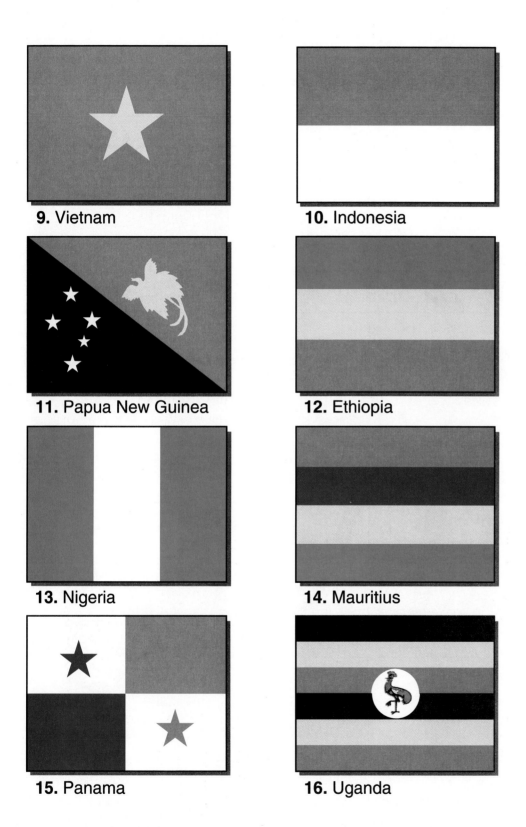

9. Vietnam

10. Indonesia

11. Papua New Guinea

12. Ethiopia

13. Nigeria

14. Mauritius

15. Panama

16. Uganda

17. *My Journal:* Design your own flag. Describe its colors
using fractional parts. Tell what is important to you
about your flag.

The Same Name

▶ Write as many equations as you can for this geoboard.

ON YOUR OWN

▶ Some VCR's provide a little picture clue that helps you estimate how much of a video has played. A thick line appears in the bottom corner of the TV screen. A small arrow moves along the line from left to right as a video plays. When a video starts, the arrow is at 0. By the time the video ends, the arrow is at 1.

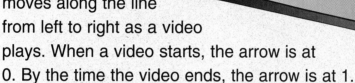

You can estimate how much of a video has played by looking at the line and estimating what fraction of it the arrow has reached. Give at least two fractions that you would use to describe where the arrow is on each line below. What clues can help? How did you decide?

1.
   0   1

2.
   0   1

3.
   0   1

4.
   0   1

5. *My Journal:* What did you learn about equivalent fractions? How could you explain what they are to someone who did not know about them? Use diagrams if you wish.

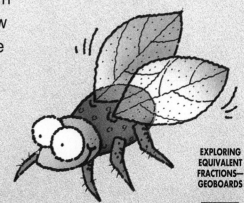

EXPLORING
EQUIVALENT
FRACTIONS—
GEOBOARDS

It's The Same!

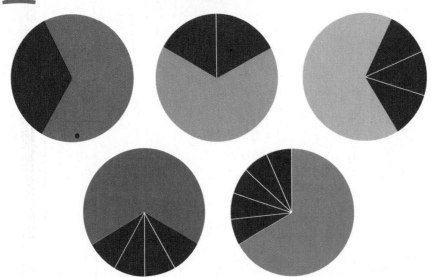

▶ What are the next three fractions equivalent to $\frac{1}{3}$?
How did you decide?

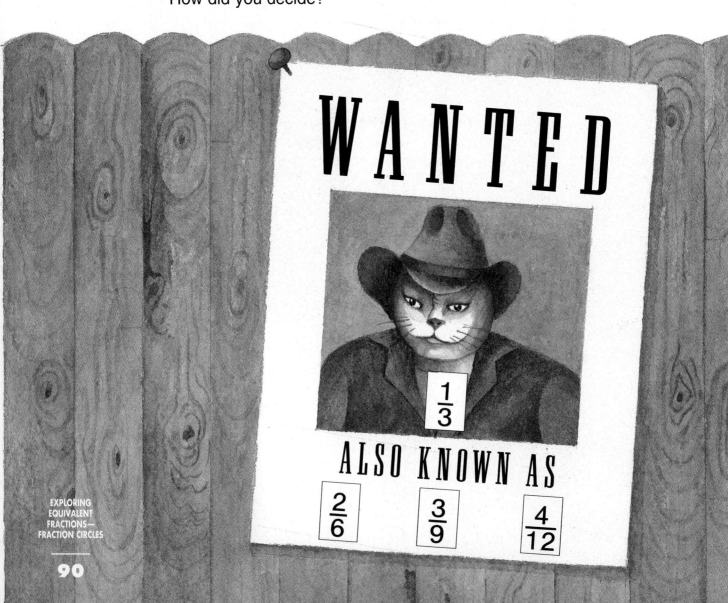

A Wall of Fractions

$\frac{1}{2}$	$\frac{1}{2}$

$\frac{1}{3}$	$\frac{1}{3}$	$\frac{1}{3}$

$\frac{1}{4}$	$\frac{1}{4}$	$\frac{1}{4}$	$\frac{1}{4}$

$\frac{1}{5}$	$\frac{1}{5}$	$\frac{1}{5}$	$\frac{1}{5}$	$\frac{1}{5}$

$\frac{1}{6}$	$\frac{1}{6}$	$\frac{1}{6}$	$\frac{1}{6}$	$\frac{1}{6}$	$\frac{1}{6}$

$\frac{1}{7}$	$\frac{1}{7}$	$\frac{1}{7}$	$\frac{1}{7}$	$\frac{1}{7}$	$\frac{1}{7}$	$\frac{1}{7}$

$\frac{1}{8}$	$\frac{1}{8}$	$\frac{1}{8}$	$\frac{1}{8}$	$\frac{1}{8}$	$\frac{1}{8}$	$\frac{1}{8}$	$\frac{1}{8}$

$\frac{1}{9}$	$\frac{1}{9}$	$\frac{1}{9}$	$\frac{1}{9}$	$\frac{1}{9}$	$\frac{1}{9}$	$\frac{1}{9}$	$\frac{1}{9}$	$\frac{1}{9}$

$\frac{1}{10}$	$\frac{1}{10}$	$\frac{1}{10}$	$\frac{1}{10}$	$\frac{1}{10}$	$\frac{1}{10}$	$\frac{1}{10}$	$\frac{1}{10}$	$\frac{1}{10}$	$\frac{1}{10}$

$\frac{1}{11}$	$\frac{1}{11}$	$\frac{1}{11}$	$\frac{1}{11}$	$\frac{1}{11}$	$\frac{1}{11}$	$\frac{1}{11}$	$\frac{1}{11}$	$\frac{1}{11}$	$\frac{1}{11}$	$\frac{1}{11}$

$\frac{1}{12}$	$\frac{1}{12}$	$\frac{1}{12}$	$\frac{1}{12}$	$\frac{1}{12}$	$\frac{1}{12}$	$\frac{1}{12}$	$\frac{1}{12}$	$\frac{1}{12}$	$\frac{1}{12}$	$\frac{1}{12}$	$\frac{1}{12}$

AMAZING
F A C T S

The Great Wall of China is about 2400 kilometers long, 5 to 15 meters high and ranges from 4 meters wide at the top to 9 meters at the base.

COMPARING
FRACTIONS

▶ Use the fraction strips on page 91 to help you solve problems 1–3.

1. Make up five questions about comparing fractions. For example, "What are the names of three fractions greater than $\frac{1}{3}$?"

2. Find at least six fractions, greater than $\frac{2}{3}$ but less than $\frac{9}{10}$.

3. Put these fractions in order from greatest to least:
$\frac{5}{4}, \frac{5}{3}, \frac{5}{8}, \frac{5}{6}, \frac{5}{5}.$

4. Estimate about what fraction of the area inside each frame is covered by the picture. Use the fractions $\frac{1}{4}, \frac{3}{4}, \frac{1}{2},$ and $\frac{1}{6}$.

5. Can $\frac{1}{2}$ ever be greater than 1 whole? Explain why or why not. Use examples to support your answer.

6. *My Journal:* What do you find easiest about comparing fractions? Why?

!Get Inside!

▶ What fraction of the pegs on the board are inside the triangle?

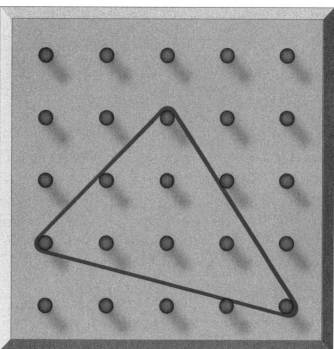

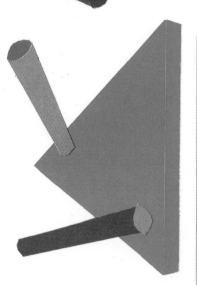

1. What is the maximum number of inside dots you can get using a triangle? Minimum number?

2. Can you make a triangle with each number of pegs inside for all numbers between the minimum and the maximum? Draw pictures to prove your conclusion.

3. *My Journal:* Do you enjoy geoboard activities? Explain.

HALF A LOAF IS BETTER THAN NONE

Have you ever wondered when fractions are necessary in every day situations?

Recipes are certainly one place, and fractions are used in recipes from around the world. You probably have tried breads from different countries. Some cities have special breads associated with them. Here is a recipe for a common bread product. Just add cream cheese!

Mystery Bread Recipe

$\frac{2}{3}$ cup milk

$\frac{1}{6}$ cup butter

$\frac{2}{3}$ tablespoon sugar

$\frac{2}{3}$ teaspoon salt

$\frac{2}{3}$ package dry yeast

2 small or 1 large egg

$2\frac{1}{2}$ cups all pupose flour sifted

2 quarts boiling water

$\frac{2}{3}$ tablespoon sugar

Scald the milk and add the next three ingredients. Use a cooking thermometer. When the temperature is about 110°F add the yeast and let it dissolve for 3 minutes. Blend in flour and eggs. Knead dough for 10 minutes adding more flour if necessary. Let the dough rise in a covered bowl until it doubles. Compact the dough and divide into 12 pieces. Roll each piece into a narrow shape about 6 inches long. Taper the ends and seal together to form the bread and cover with a cloth. Let the dough rise for about 15 minutes. Drop one-by-one into the boiling water to which $\frac{2}{3}$ tablespoon of sugar has been added. As the bread pieces rise to the surface turn them and cook for 3–4 minutes. Take them from the water and bake on a cookie sheet in preheated oven at 400°F for 25 minutes.

1 What bread is the recipe for? Can you find recipes for other types?

2 Does your family use any special breads? Can you find a recipe to share? What fractions are in the recipe?

3 Which breads might be difficult to divide in parts? Which would be easy?

4 Find a recipe for your favorite bread. Adjust it so you could make enough for your class.

Dogs Love Fractions!

▶ A recent survey found that 1 out of 4 dog owners in the United States celebrate their dog's birthday.

▶ Of the people who celebrate their dog's birthday, 2 out of 5 give the dog a special treat.

1. What fraction of the masks are painted? What fraction of the masks have feathers? What fraction of the masks are worn to protect the face from injury?

FRACTIONS OF SETS-UNLIKE ELEMENTS

2. Think about the people in your household. What fractional part of your household is male? What fraction is female? What fractional part of your household is over 18? What fraction is under 18?

3. *Math* is a word that is $\frac{3}{4}$ consonants and $\frac{1}{4}$ vowels. Think of three other words you can describe as $\frac{3}{4}$ consonants and $\frac{1}{4}$ vowels. Think of some words that are $\frac{3}{5}$ consonants and $\frac{2}{5}$ vowels. How would you describe your own name?

4. The United States is a group of 50 states, 1 territory, and 1 district. Canada is a group of 10 provinces and 2 territories. Mexico is a group of 29 states and 2 territories. Pick one of these countries. Find a map of it in an atlas, encyclopedia, or other book. Use the map to write some fraction statements about the country. Find what fraction of the states, provinces, territories, or districts:

   a. border a foreign country.   **b.** begin with N.

   c. border an ocean.   **d.** border the Great Lakes.

   Then answer these questions:

   e. Do you think it is correct to say that any one state, province, territory, or district is $\frac{1}{51}$, $\frac{1}{12}$, or $\frac{1}{31}$ of the whole country? Explain.

   f. Find your own state, province, district, or territory. Does it cover $\frac{1}{52}$, $\frac{1}{12}$, or $\frac{1}{31}$ of your whole country? Estimate the fraction of the area of your country you think it does cover.

5. *My Journal:* What have you learned about fractional parts of sets? Explain.

It's All Mixed Up!

▶ Here's what to do:

1. Find some classroom objects to measure with your strip of paper.

2. Before you measure, estimate the length of the objects. Record using fractions or mixed numbers.

3. Measure each object and record your measurement using fractions or mixed numbers.

MEASURING CLASSROOM OBJECTS		
Object	**Estimate**	**Length**
Book	1 Strip	$1\frac{3}{4}$ Strips

How Long?

► What does each mark mean on the measuring tape?

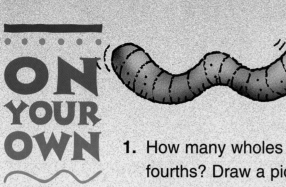

ON YOUR OWN

1. How many wholes do you have if you have thirteen fourths? Draw a picture to explain. What mixed number names the picture?

2. Draw squares to show $2\frac{1}{8}$. How many eighths is this in all?

3. Which is more, $\frac{3}{4}$ or $\frac{4}{3}$? How do you know?

4. Can you show at least five ways to write $2\frac{1}{2}$?

5. Copy these rectangles. How many thirds can be made from these 3 wholes?

6. If you earned a quarter for every 15 minutes you worked, how many quarters would you have after $3\frac{1}{2}$ hours? How many dollars?

7. Jacey measured her shoe and found it was $7\frac{3}{4}$ inches long. When Frank measured it, he said it was $7\frac{6}{8}$ inches long. How can this be?

8. *My Journal:* Write and explain what you have learned about mixed numbers. How can mixed numbers help you when you measure?

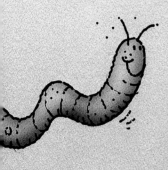

Make a Two-Loop Glide

Here's what to do:

1. Measure and cut two $8\frac{1}{2}$-inch long strips of paper. Make one strip $1\frac{3}{4}$ inches wide and the other $\frac{3}{4}$ of an inch wide.

2. Bring both ends of each strip together to form two loops. Overlap the ends and tape them together on both sides.

3. Line up one end of the straw with the edge of the wide loop. Tape the straw to the inside of the loop, on the overlap to form the back loop of the glider.

4. Put the narrow loop on the other end of the straw. Let the straw stick out past the front edge of the loop at least $\frac{1}{2}$ inch, but not more than $1\frac{1}{2}$ inches. Tape the straw to the inside of the loop, on the overlap.

Glider Flying Competition

1. Decide on and mark off a playing field.

2. Establish boundaries and a starting line.

3. Your feet must be behind the starting line when you launch your glider.

4. Launch your glider.

5. If your glider goes out of bounds, you can launch it again.

6. If your glider lands in bounds, estimate the distance it flew to the nearest $\frac{1}{4}$ foot. Use the front of the glider to estimate. Record the distance.

7. Decide how many turns everyone gets before a winner is declared.

*Check*YOURSELF

Great job! Your glider is correctly constructed. You followed all the directions in the proper order. After testing, you made some adjustments and then your glider was able to fly farther. You used fractions and described your work with them correctly.

*H*ow can we show and use decimals?

Two Halves Make a Whole

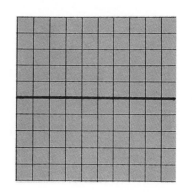

$\frac{1}{2}$

▶ What other fraction could you use to describe $\frac{1}{2}$ of the square?

How did you decide?

Could you show halves of each figure in other ways?

1. Divide a 10 x 10 grid into 10 equal sections. Shade 3 of these sections. Write two equivalent fractions for the shaded region. Explain why you wrote those fractions.

2. Use two 10 x 10 grids. Shade $\frac{4}{10}$ on one grid and $\frac{40}{100}$ on the other. What do you notice about the shaded regions?

3. Which is greater, $\frac{35}{100}$ or $\frac{7}{10}$? Prove your answer using 10 x 10 grids.

Refer to the figure at the right for problems 4-6.

4. How many long orange blocks are needed to completely cover the 10 x 10 grid? How many white blocks are needed?

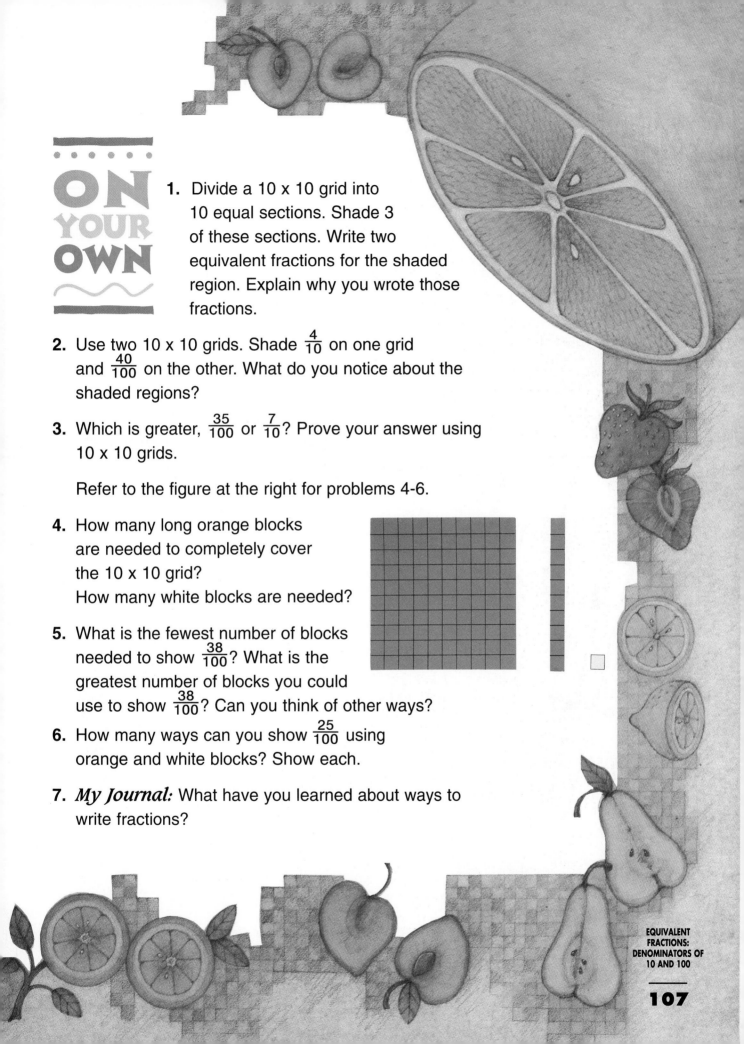

5. What is the fewest number of blocks needed to show $\frac{38}{100}$? What is the greatest number of blocks you could use to show $\frac{38}{100}$? Can you think of other ways?

6. How many ways can you show $\frac{25}{100}$ using orange and white blocks? Show each.

7. *My Journal:* What have you learned about ways to write fractions?

Press-to, Change-O!

During this activity, you will be using a decimal ring and a calculator to find decimals that are equivalent to unit fractions. You may find it helpful to record your work in a table similar to the one shown below.

▶ Follow these steps to use your calculator to find the decimal equivalent to $\frac{1}{2}$.

A. Enter 1.   **B.** Press / .   **C.** Enter 2.   **D.** Press F$\circlearrowright$D.

UNIT FRACTION	EQUIVALENT FRACTION TENTHS	EQUIVALENT FRACTION HUNDREDTHS	DECIMAL ON RING	DECIMAL ON CALCULATOR
$\frac{1}{2}$	$\frac{5}{10}$	$\frac{50}{100}$	0.50	0.5

ON YOUR OWN

▶ Use your fraction pieces, decimal ring, calculator, or any method you want to solve these problems.

1. Match each fraction with its decimal equivalent. Then write your matching pairs in order from least to greatest. Explain how you did this.

$\frac{1}{4}$	0.20
$\frac{1}{8}$	0.10
$\frac{1}{2}$	0.25
$\frac{1}{3}$	0.125
$\frac{1}{10}$	0.3333333
$\frac{1}{5}$	0.50

2. *My Journal:* How are decimals related to fractions?

Find That Decimal!

▶ Can you find decimal equivalents for these fractions?

$$\frac{2}{3} \quad \frac{3}{4} \quad \frac{2}{5} \quad \frac{3}{8} \quad \frac{4}{6} \quad \frac{8}{10}$$

Ways to Find Equivalents

1. Estimate whether the decimal equivalent for each fraction is closest to 0, 0.25, 0.50, 0.75 or 1. Use your recording sheet from Activity 2 to help you with this.

2. Use fractions pieces and a decimal ring to find each decimal equivalent. It may be a decimal or an estimate.

3. Use your calculator to find an exact decimal equivalent for each fraction. Record exactly what is shown on the calculator display.

What patterns do you see?

Write about them.

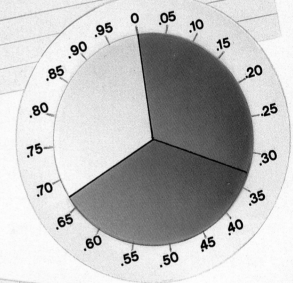

FRACTION	DECIMAL ESTIMATE	DECIMAL ON RING	DECIMAL ON CALCULATOR
2/3	0.75	BETWEEN 0.65 + 0.70	0.6666667

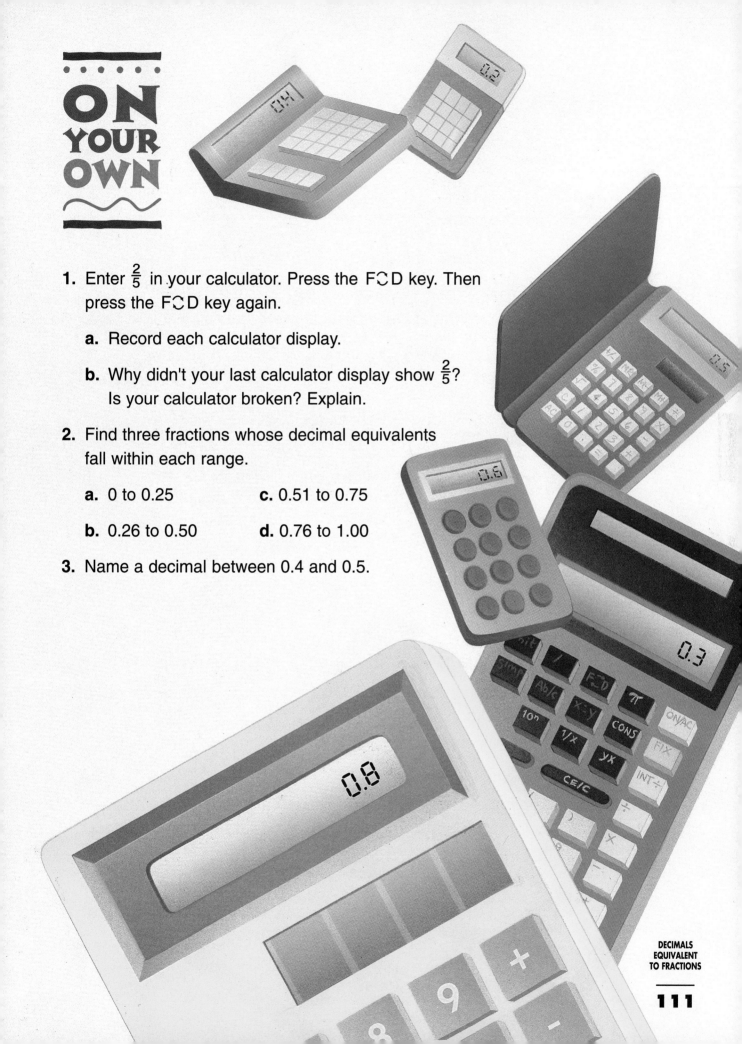

ON YOUR OWN

1. Enter $\frac{2}{5}$ in your calculator. Press the F⊃D key. Then press the F⊃D key again.

   a. Record each calculator display.

   b. Why didn't your last calculator display show $\frac{2}{5}$? Is your calculator broken? Explain.

2. Find three fractions whose decimal equivalents fall within each range.

   a. 0 to 0.25   c. 0.51 to 0.75

   b. 0.26 to 0.50   d. 0.76 to 1.00

3. Name a decimal between 0.4 and 0.5.

ON YOUR OWN

4. Name a decimal between 0.76 and 0.77.

5. The decimal approximation for $\frac{11}{12}$ is 0.9166667. Between what decimals on the decimal ring is this?

6. Explain how you can tell just by looking that $\frac{15}{24}$ is greater than 0.5.

7. Prove that $\frac{2}{5}$ is less than 0.5 without using a calculator.

8. *My Journal:* Explain two ways to find a decimal equivalent to a given fraction. Which is easier for you? Why?

Order, Please

about 0.6666667   0.40

$\frac{2}{3}$ is greater than $\frac{2}{5}$.

0.6666667 is greater than 0.40.

1. Write these in order from least to greatest. Write and explain how you decided on your order.

$\frac{3}{5}$ $\frac{99}{100}$ 0.25 $\frac{7}{12}$ 0.75   0.49

2. Which is larger: 0.02 or 0.2? Prove it.

3. Write these in order from least to greatest. If any are equal, write them one above the other. Write and tell how you decided. Prove your answer is correct by drawing pictures.

3.0   0.03   0.3   0.30

4. Use the digits 3 and 4 to write a decimal that is between 0.4 and 0.5. Write and tell how you decided.

5. Copy the numbers. Place a decimal point in the middle number so that the numbers are in order from least to greatest. Write and tell how you decided.

7   78   8

6. Write as many decimals as you can in one minute that are between 0.6 and 0.7.

7. *My Journal:* What questions do you have about ordering decimals?

Let's Go on a Meter Hunt!

▶ Find five objects in your classroom that you estimate to be less than 1 meter long or tall.

Estimate the length of each in centimeters.

Then use a meter tape or stick to find each actual measurement to the nearest centimeter.

Finally, write each measurement as a decimal in meters.

You may want to record your work on a sheet like this:

| OBJECT | ESTIMATED LENGTH | ACTUAL LENGTH IN | |
		CENTIMETERS	METERS
Chair Back	80 cm		

MEASURING
OBJECTS LESS THAN
1 METER LONG

115

GETTING YOUR

BITS IN

quarter
$ .25

half dollar
$ .50

Spanish
real

Have you ever wondered whether money from other countries is like our money in the United States? The money system in the United States is a decimal or base ten system. However we also use fractions to refer to some of our money.

The early Spaniards used fractions. In 18th century Spain the unit of currency was the silver real. (ray-AHL) An 8-real coin was often physically cut into pieces. A convenient piece was the $\frac{2}{8}$ piece called two bits. Since the Spanish 8-real coin was sometimes called a Spanish dollar, the slang term 2 bits is used to describe our quarter.

The British system of money used fractional relationships for many years. The British system was based on pounds, shilling, and pence and had these equivalencies:

1 pound = 20 shillings

1 shilling = 12 pence

In 1971 the British switched to a decimal system and eliminated the shilling. Now 1 pound = 100 pence.

Decimals are used in foreign currency tables in newspapers and banks but people often use fractional approximations saying, for example, "The Canadian dollar is worth $\frac{3}{4}$ of the U. S. dollar," or "The Mexican peso is worth about $\frac{1}{3}$ of a dollar."

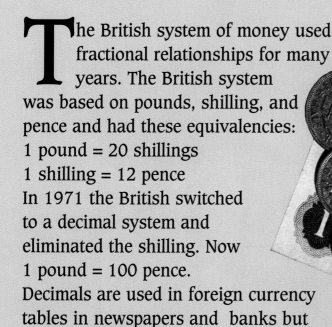

1. Was the pence a bigger or smaller fraction of the pound in the old British system? Explain your reasoning. Could you tell if it was actually worth more or less? What would you need to know?

2. Do you or your family have coins from another country? How could you find out what they are worth in relation to the U.S. dollar?

3. Make up your own money system. What will your unit be? What will parts of your unit be? Will your system be based on decimals or fractions?

Reach!

▶ Do you agree with each of these statements? Explain.

Your arm reach is about 44 cm or 0.44 m.

I can reach that 2 m high shelf, so my arm reach must be 2 m.

ON YOUR OWN

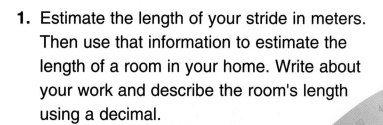

1. Estimate the length of your stride in meters. Then use that information to estimate the length of a room in your home. Write about your work and describe the room's length using a decimal.

2. Choose four family members, friends, or neighbors. Suppose they all stood side by side with their arms stretched out on both sides. Estimate how long that line would be. Write a description of your work.

3. *My Journal:* Why are decimals helpful in measuring?

MEASURING
OBJECTS
GREATER THAN
1 METER LONG

Designing TABLES

Design a table that will seat you and 5 of your classmates. Draw a plan for building your table. Then write a report describing your work.

Here are some things to think about:

- What shape table do you want?
- What would you use the table for?
- What else should you consider?

PLAN

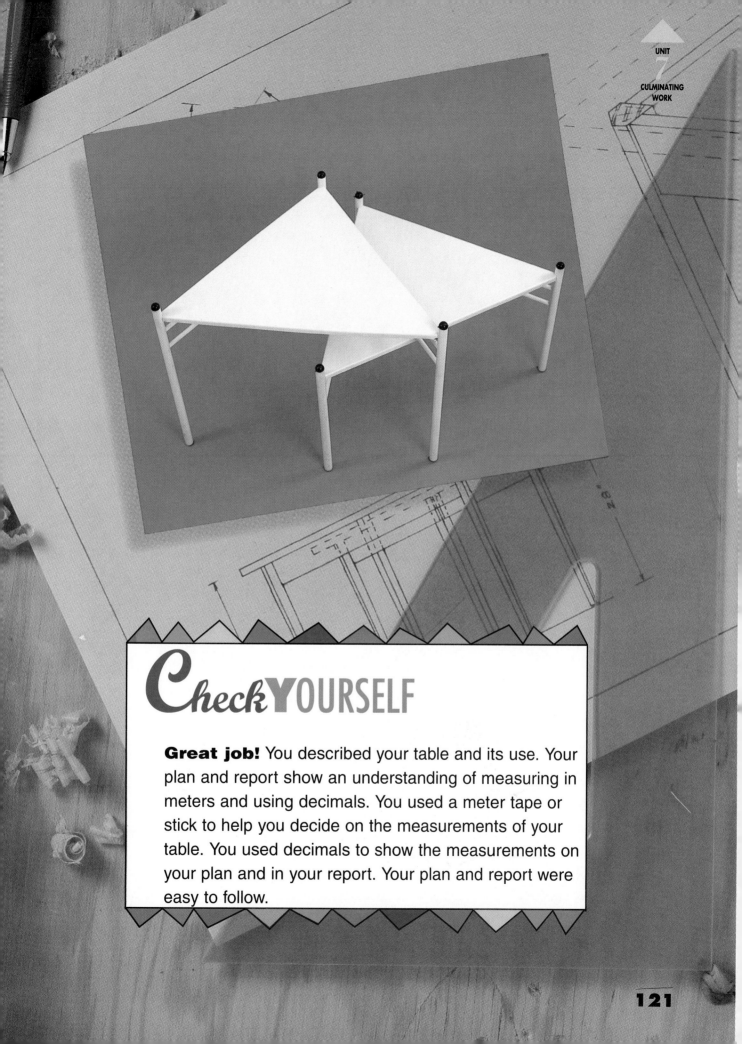

Check YOURSELF

Great job! You described your table and its use. Your plan and report show an understanding of measuring in meters and using decimals. You used a meter tape or stick to help you decide on the measurements of your table. You used decimals to show the measurements on your plan and in your report. Your plan and report were easy to follow.

*H*ow can polygons be combined?

In the Fold

▶ You will need several paper squares. Try to fold one square of the paper to make each set of shapes shown. Draw lines on each square to show the folds.

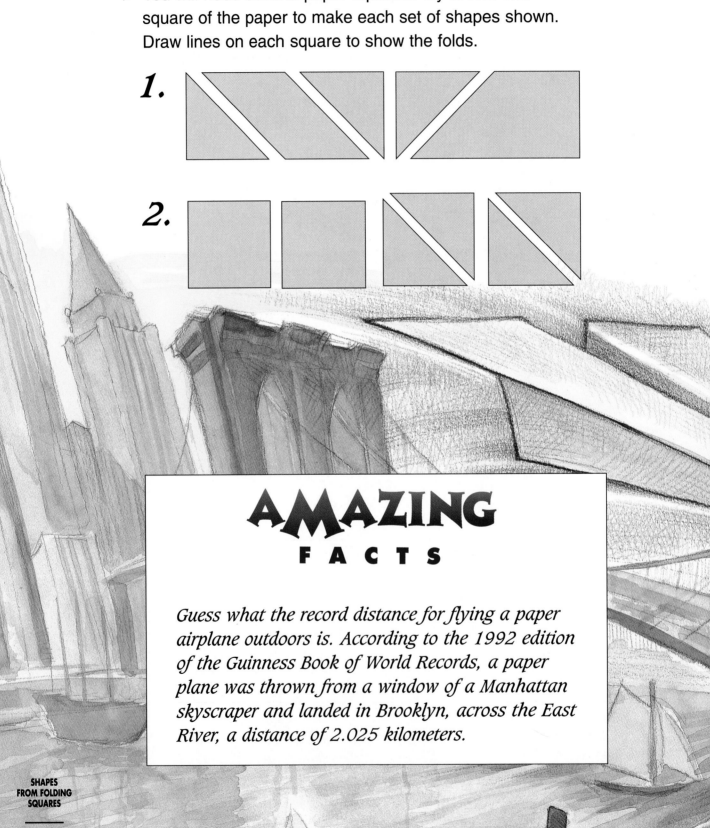

1.

2.

AMAZING
F A C T S

Guess what the record distance for flying a paper airplane outdoors is. According to the 1992 edition of the Guinness Book of World Records, a paper plane was thrown from a window of a Manhattan skyscraper and landed in Brooklyn, across the East River, a distance of 2.025 kilometers.

ON YOUR OWN

1. Follow the paper-folding steps to make a square puzzle.

Step 1

Fold on this dotted line.

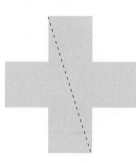

Step 2

Fold on this dotted line.

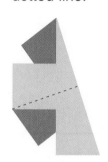

Step 3

Cut on this dotted line.

2. Do you think you can put these shapes back together to make a square? Try it and show your results.

3. *My Journal:* What shapes can be made by combining equilateral triangles?

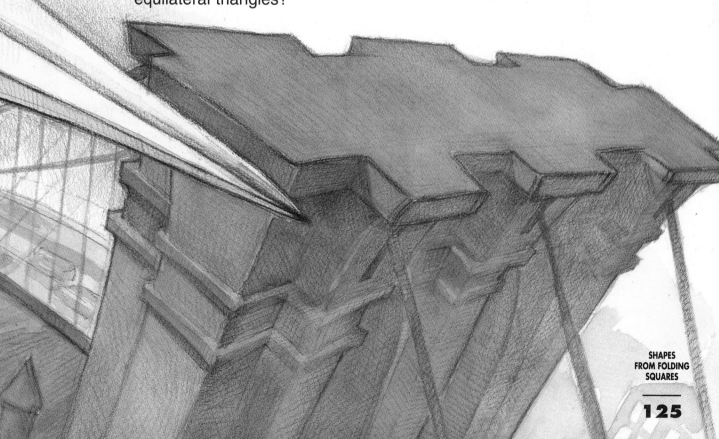

 Tangram Puzzler

The seven tangram pieces fit together to make a square puzzle. This is what it looks like:

► You can fold a paper square to make the puzzle.
Here are the steps to do it.

Make a diagonal fold.

1.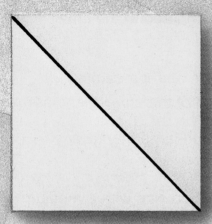

Bring one corner to
the diagonal fold. Crease.

2.

Make the other diagonal.
Crease part way, as shown.

3.

Bring the corner toward the
center to make the crease shown.

4.

Fold one side toward the center.
Crease as shown.

5.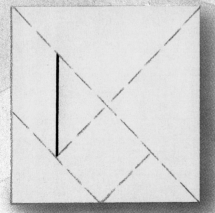

Try it again.
Can you do it
without the directions?

Area Undercover

▶ Use your set of tangram pieces, and your answers to the questions below, to help you come to some conclusions.

1. How big is a small triangle compared to the small square? How can you tell?

2. If you think of the small square as representing 1 square unit, how big is each of the small triangles?

3. How do the small, medium, and large triangles compare in size?

4. How does the square compare in size with a medium triangle? With a large triangle? How do you know?

5. How does the parallelogram compare in size with each of the other pieces?

▶ Now use your tangram pieces to solve these problems.

6. Make as many combinations of triangles as you can. What is the area of each?

7. What is the area of the largest square you can make?

▶ Make a chart that shows the relationships of the sizes of the tangram pieces. Use the small square as 1 unit square.

Then use your set of pieces to create the shapes described below, and to answer the questions about your shapes.

1. Make a figure with an area of 6 square units. How did you do it? What is another way to do it? How do you know?

2. Make an evergreen tree. What is its area?

3. Make a house. Then make a house with a bigger area. How much larger is the area of the bigger one?

4. Make a letter of the alphabet. How did you do it? What is its area?

5. Make another letter with the same area. How do you know the two letters have the same area?

6. Choose a size. Create a shape exactly that size. Then make another shape that has the same area. How did you do it?

7. *My Journal:* For which shapes was it easiest for you to find the area? Explain why.

COMBINING POLYGONS IN SPACE

D id you ever wonder what kinds of three dimensional figures you could make by combining polygons? Long ago the people from Egypt and Greece found these space figures very interesting. They studied their properties and found relationships among the sides, faces and vertices.

Here are patterns or nets for two space figures made from polygons that you can make.
Trace each pattern or net and make the space figure.

Alexandrian icosahedron
(many sided number cube)

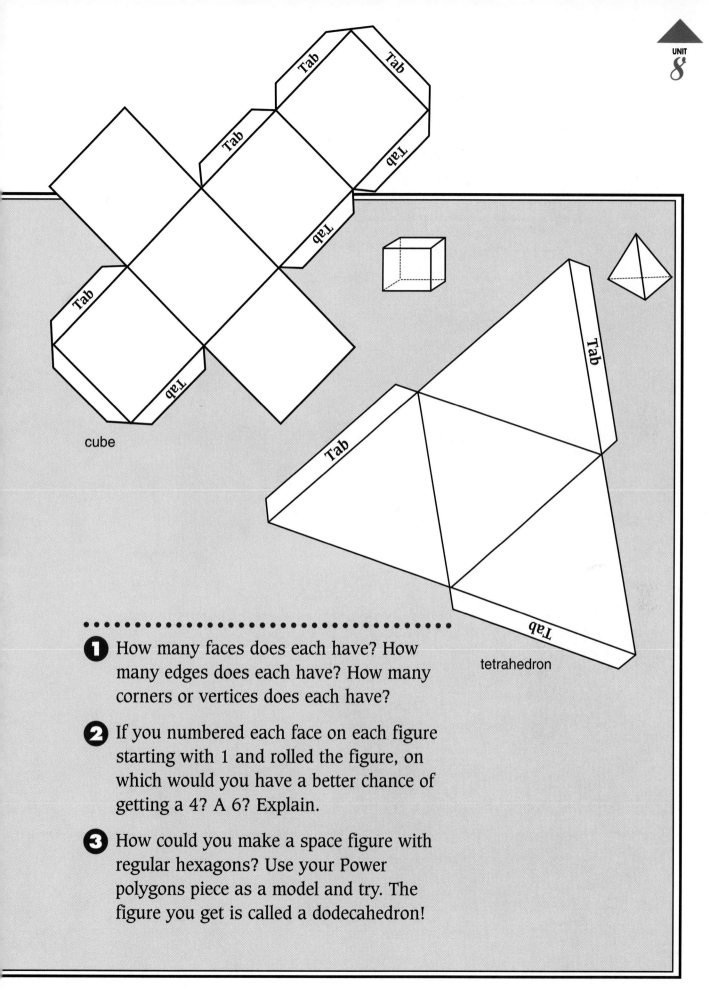

cube

tetrahedron

1 How many faces does each have? How many edges does each have? How many corners or vertices does each have?

2 If you numbered each face on each figure starting with 1 and rolled the figure, on which would you have a better chance of getting a 4? A 6? Explain.

3 How could you make a space figure with regular hexagons? Use your Power polygons piece as a model and try. The figure you get is called a dodecahedron!

131

Tangram Cover-Up

▶ Use your tangram pieces to make the figures on these pages. Those on this page can be made with all seven pieces. Some of the figures on the facing page can be made with fewer than seven pieces. Some can be made in more than one way.

Under Cover

▶ Use your tangram pieces to try to make figures with the same shape as those on this page.

Are there any you can't make?

Explain why you can't. Describe or draw the additional pieces you would need.

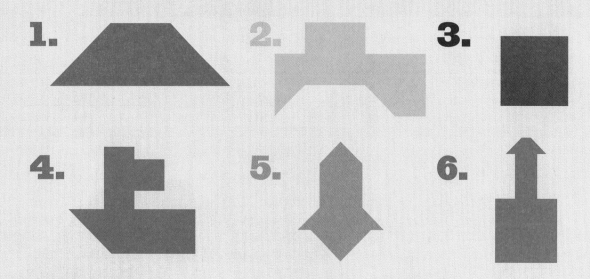

1.   2.   3.

4.   5.   6.

ON YOUR OWN

Use your tangram pieces to create two different figures someone would recognize, such as an animal, a letter or number, a truck, a boat, and so on.

Draw only the outline of each figure. On the back of the page, name each figure and show with dotted lines how you made it.

Exchange your figures with other students. See if anyone can identify your figures, and if she or he can make them in different ways.

My Journal: What have you learned about tangrams?

Reflecting on Shapes

ON YOUR OWN

1. Can you continue to make larger and larger triangles that look the same? Make a table that allows you to predict the number of triangles you will need to make larger and larger triangles that are similar to your original triangle.

   Share your table and conclusions with classmates.

 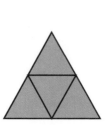 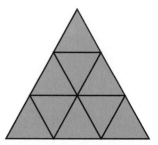

2. Can you make a table to show the pattern for squares?

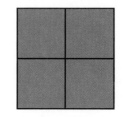 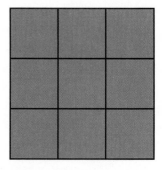

3. Can you make a table to show the pattern for hexagons? Remember to use trapezoids.

 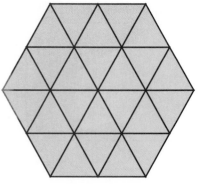

4. *My Journal:* Share whether you found this activity interesting. Why or why not?

Calling All Squares

A pentomino is formed by combining five squares, each the same size. The squares meet along the sides so that each square shares a side with at least one other square.

This is a pentomino.   This isn't.

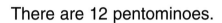

There are 12 pentominoes.

▶ Use your color tiles. Try to make all 12 pentominoes without looking back at this page until you finish.

ON YOUR OWN

Each rectangle below contains all 12 pentominoes. The first one is 4 squares high and 15 across. The second one is 6 squares across and 10 high.

1. Try to make each rectangle without looking back to this page until you finish. Use your color tiles or sketch with your pencil on grid paper. Then check your answers.

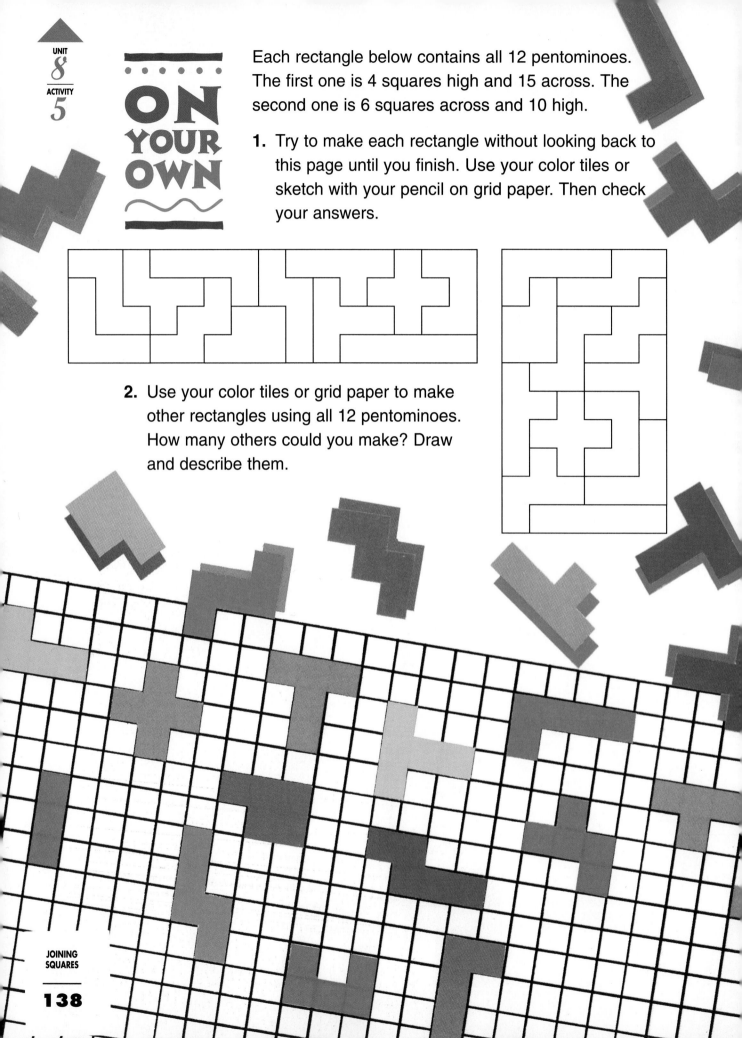

2. Use your color tiles or grid paper to make other rectangles using all 12 pentominoes. How many others could you make? Draw and describe them.

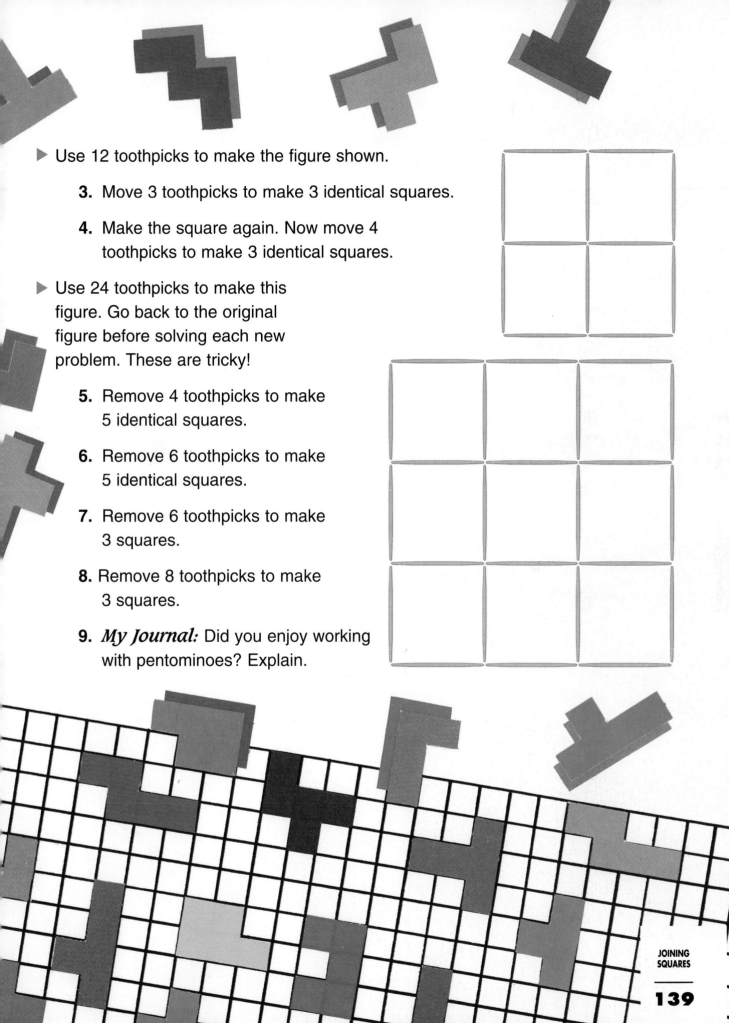

▶ Use 12 toothpicks to make the figure shown.

3. Move 3 toothpicks to make 3 identical squares.

4. Make the square again. Now move 4 toothpicks to make 3 identical squares.

▶ Use 24 toothpicks to make this figure. Go back to the original figure before solving each new problem. These are tricky!

5. Remove 4 toothpicks to make 5 identical squares.

6. Remove 6 toothpicks to make 5 identical squares.

7. Remove 6 toothpicks to make 3 squares.

8. Remove 8 toothpicks to make 3 squares.

9. *My Journal:* Did you enjoy working with pentominoes? Explain.

Joining Together

▶ Use your Power Polygons.
Find as many ways as you can
to join triangles and hexagons
edge to edge. Record the figures
you make.

1

In how many ways can you join
2 triangles? 3 triangles?

2

In how many ways can you
join 4, 5, and 6 triangles?

3

In how many ways can you join 2
hexagons? 3 hexagons?
4 hexagons? Record all the
different figures you can make.

ON YOUR OWN

1. Examine this figure. How would you describe it? Make the shape with toothpicks.

   a. Move 4 toothpicks to make 3 equilateral triangles.

   b. Put the toothpicks back where they were. Now move 4 toothpicks to make 4 identical diamonds.

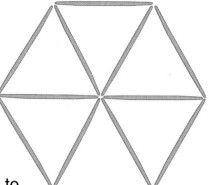

2. Regular hexagons can be joined at their edges to make patterns. Look at the two photos.

   a. What can you say about these patterns?

   b. What other shapes do you think can make patterns like these? Try out your predictions using dot paper or grid paper.

   c. Do you think regular pentagons could be joined at their edges to make patterns? Try to find out.

3. *My Journal:* What did you learn about joining triangles and hexagons? Which figure was more interesting?

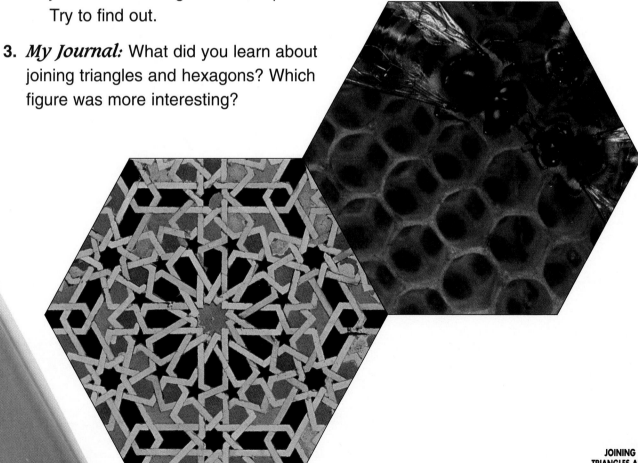

JOINING TRIANGLES AND HEXAGONS

Changing
SHAPES

Here is a puzzle made by dividing a large square into smaller polygons. Trace the square and cut out the pieces. Rearrange them to form three smaller squares of equal size. Can you make the large square again?

Create a new puzzle of your own that is made up of smaller parts.

Hints: Think about what the tangram puzzles and the pentomino puzzles had in common. Think about the puzzle on the previous page that you just solved.

1. Begin by drawing a plan for your design. Use Power Polygons of grid paper as needed.

2. Cut out your pieces and solve your puzzle.

3. Draw a picture of the pieces and the solution to your puzzle.

4. Record the steps in the solution.

5. Swap puzzles with a classmate. Try to solve each other's puzzles.

6. What hints would you give someone trying to solve your puzzle?

7. Write a description of the experience of making and solving the puzzles. What was the hardest? What was easiest? What was the most fun?

CheckYOURSELF

Great job! You made a good plan and followed it. Your puzzle was carefully drawn. The puzzle pieces fit together to make a new shape. The puzzle was interesting for other students to work—but not too hard! You described in writing how you made the puzzle and how to solve it.

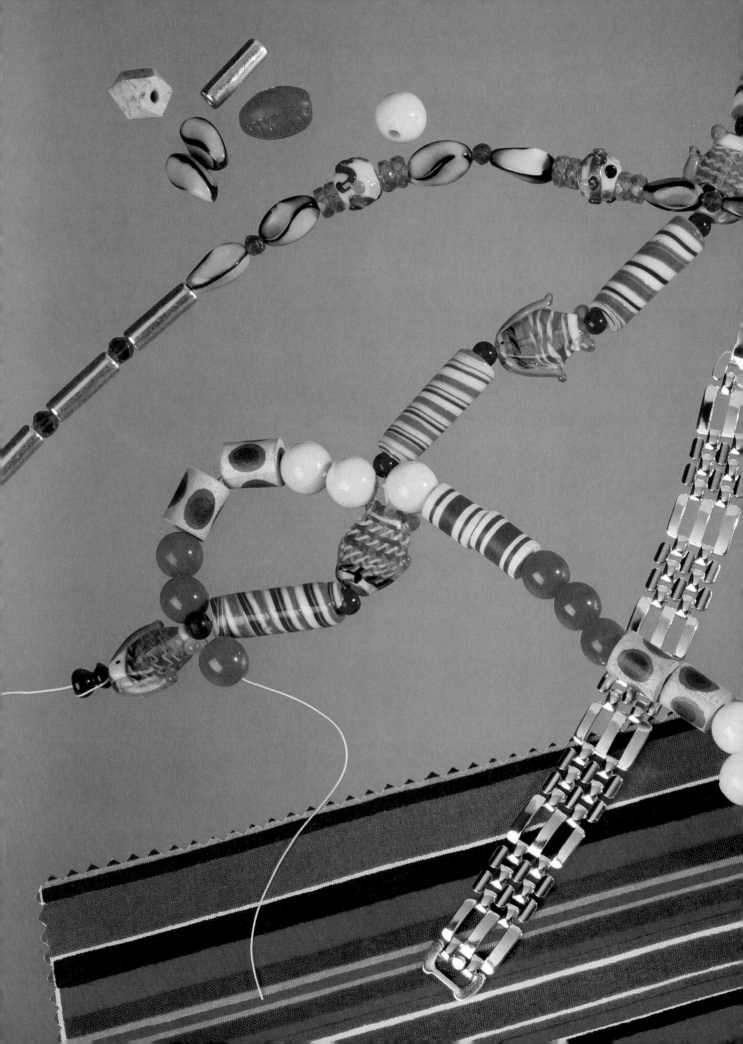

*H*ow can we
use patterns
to predict?

UNIT 9 ACTIVITY 1

Castle Walls

Use models and complete the T-tables to answer each of the questions.

1. How many pieces do you need to build a castle wall with 6 towers?

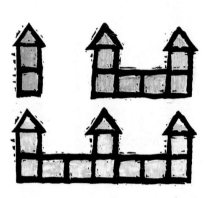

Number of Towers	Number of Pieces
1	3
2	8
3	13
4	?
5	?
6	?

2. How many pieces do you need to build a 5-tower wall?

Number of Towers	Number of Pieces
1	2
2	5
3	8
4	?
5	?
6	?

3. How many towers are in a 36-piece wall?

Number of Towers	Number of Pieces
1	4
2	12
3	20
4	?
5	?
6	?

DESCRIBING A PATTERN

146

1. How many Power Polygons does it take to make a design with 10 green triangles?

Triangles	Power Polygons
1	3
2	5
3	7
4	?

2. Think up a pattern using clapping. Begin your pattern. Ask a family member to clap to continue your pattern. Try another one. Then switch roles. Describe your pattern in words and make a T-table for it.

CLAPS
long	short
2	3
4	6
6	?

4. Look together around your home for examples of patterns like the ones in this activity. Can you make a table for them? Describe the patterns you find.

5. *My Journal:* Do you enjoy making and recording patterns? Explain.

AMAZING
F A C T S

Castle walls can be several feet thick, and the thickest walls ever were those of the ancient city of Ur in today's Iraq. Its mud brick walls were 88 feet thick!

NOTES ON
Computers

Dr. Donna Auguste

Have you ever wondered how patterns are used in music? Or in computers? Both African Americans and American Indians have long musical traditions that use interesting and complex rhythmic patterns, but many have never been written down. With new technological developments, computers can be used to write some of these musical patterns.

Dr. Donna Auguste, who is an African-American and American-Indian woman, led the team which designed a hand-held, pen-based computer that recognizes handwriting patterns and converts them to typed text. She is also a musician interested in translating African-American and American-Indian musical patterns to written notes. Dr. Auguste turns song into writing when she creates arrangements for her gospel choir with her computer.

African American
gospel singers
in choir

1 Look in a music text or at a
piece of sheet music. What
patterns do you see? What
systems are used to show how
high or low a note is? how
long or short its duration is?

2 Listen to music of different
types and from different
cultures. What patterns do
you hear? How would you
show or explain those
patterns to someone?

3 Play a piece of your favorite
music on a recorder or other
clasroom instrument.
What patterns can your
classmates hear?

149

Tables and Toothpicks

Use models and complete the T-tables
to answer each of the questions.

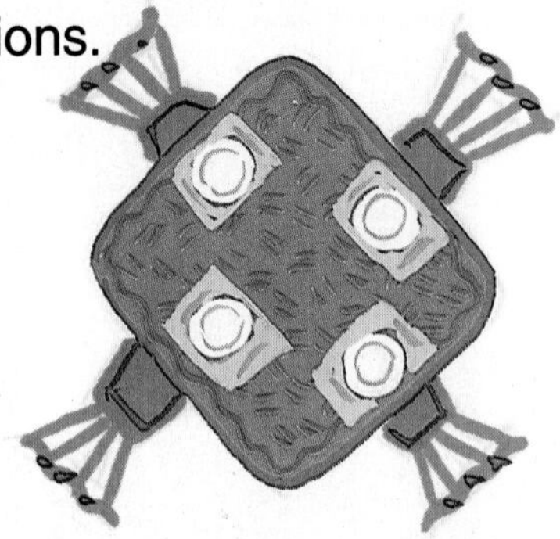

This table seats 4.

How many people can be
seated when 8 tables are
placed in a row?

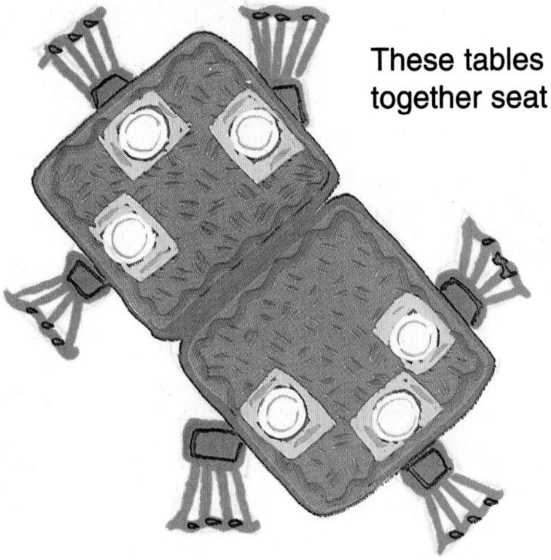

These tables
together seat 6.

Number of Tables	Number of People Seated
1	4
2	6
3	8
4	?

How many toothpicks
are needed for 4 triangles?
For 6 triangles?

With 3 toothpicks
you can make
1 triangle. You
need 5 to
make 2
triangles.

Number of Triangles	Number of Toothpicks
1	3
2	5
3	7
4	?
5	?
6	?

1. Suppose you need to seat 22 people at square tables placed end-to-end. The tables seat 1 person on a side, to make one big table. How many tables do you need? Explain your plan.

2. Suppose you had 17 toothpicks to continue the triangle design on page 150. Your design left off at 6 triangles. How many triangles can you build? Explain your thinking.

3. *My Journal:* Did you prefer the table or the toothpick problem? Explain why.

AMAZING
F A C T S

You can make an amazing toothpick puzzle. Arrange 40 toothpicks as shown. How many squares can you see? Look for small, medium, large, and extra-large squares. Then try to remove 9 toothpicks so that there are no squares left at all.

CHAIN PATTERNS

How does the perimeter change as the chain gets longer?

Number of Triangles	Perimeter
1	3
2	4
3	5
4	?
5	?
6	?
7	?
8	?
9	?
10	?

Now choose two shapes other than a triangle to investigate. How does the perimeter change as a chain of shapes gets longer? Here are some things to think about.

- Do you think the patterns will be the same as for triangles? Why or why not?
- How can a T-table help you predict what happens?
- How many rows will the T-table need before you can make a good prediction?

CheckYOURSELF

Great job! You created a polygon chain pattern. Your T-table accurately showed what happened as the chains of shapes got longer. You used the T-tables to make and test some predictions about how the perimeter changes. You identified the patterns and were sure they would work for any number of shapes. You wrote to describe clearly the patterns.

What are
the
chances?

155

here Will it Stop?

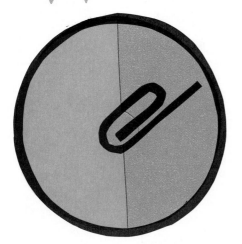

How many times out of 100 spins might you get orange? Why?

▶ Follow these directions:

1 Use the Spinner Circle and a paper clip to make a spinner with two colors so that you might expect to get one of the colors 70 out of 100 spins.

2 Write and tell why you think your spinner will give 70 out of 100 of one color.

3 Do 100 trials with your spinner. Record your findings. Did you get 70 out of 100 of one color?

4 Would you like to try again? If so, use the results from your first spinner to draw another spinner.

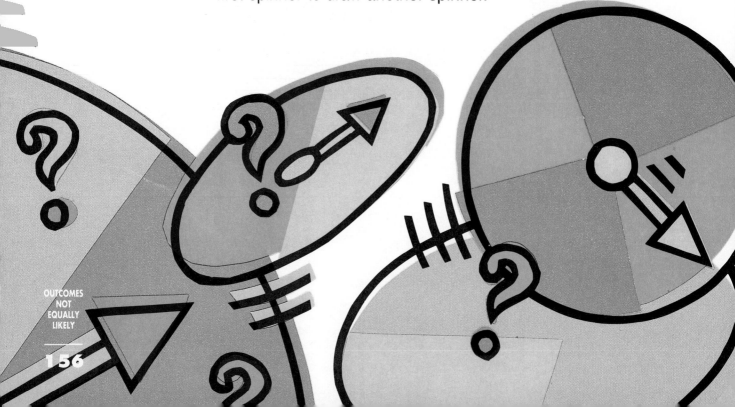

1. In 100 spins of this spinner, how many oranges do you predict you will get? How many golds? Explain your thinking. If the same spinner were spun 500 times, how many of each color do you predict you would get? Explain.

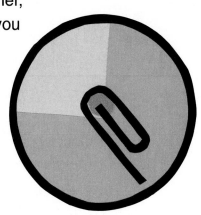

For problems 2, 3, and 4 write the number of times you predict each color will come up in 1,000 spins. Tell how you decided.

2.

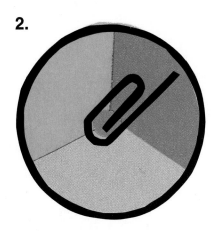

3.

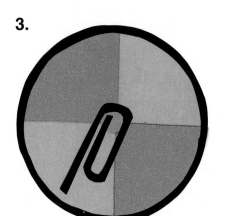

4.

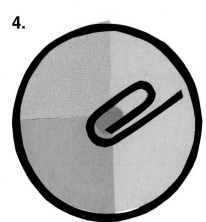

For problems 5, 6, and 7 draw a spinner that you think will give the results shown.

5. 55 orange
45 green
in 100 spins

6. 200 blue
300 orange
in 500 spins

7. 600 gold
300 blue
100 red
in 1,000 spins

8. *My Journal:* What did you learn that was new?

OUTCOMES
NOT
EQUALLY
LIKELY

What's Your Prediction?

Materials

• •

1 clear plastic cup
1 rubber band
1 sheet of plastic wrap
10 folded pieces of construction paper

1 Place the folded papers in the cup. Cover the cup with the plastic and secure using the rubber band.

2 Copy the chart shown below.

Possible Outcome	My Prediction	Tally	Actual Outcome
fold down			
fold up			

3 Predict the number of times you believe each outcome will occur in 100 trials (taken 10 at a time). Record your predictions in the chart.

4 Shake the cup, remove the wrap and toss the papers on your desk .

5 Mark a tally for each of the 10 folded papers with the appropriate outcome.

6 Repeat the experiment 9 more times for a total of 100 outcomes.

Conduct 50 trials of each experiment below. For each experiment, make a chart like the one on page 158. Then write a sentence to describe the chance of each outcome occurring.

1. Bend a paper clip as shown and toss it.

2. Toss a bottle cap or shaving cream can cap.

3. Label the sides of a flat eraser 1 and 2 and toss it.

4. *My Journal:* Explain what you know about equally likely and not equally likely outcomes.

SKILL OR LUCK?

Have you ever wondered what kinds of games of chance people play? The game of Churchurki was played by American Indians. Two teams of 4 players sat opposite each other. Each player hid a small black reed in one hand and a small white reed in the other. The first player on one team guessed in which hand the first player of the other team held the white reed. If the guess was correct, the guessing team got 3 tokens. Then the other team got a turn to guess. The first team to get 15 tokens won.

The game of ball drop is another game that was played by American Indians. In this game a wooden ball, 1 inch in diameter, or a pebble is dropped by an extended arm at shoulder height into a shell, 3 inches in diameter. The goal is to drop the object into the shell so that it goes inside and remains inside. Each player gets 3 turns.

You can play both of these games. For Churchurki use two different colored tiles or counters. For the ball drop use a small sponge or paper ball and a deep paper cup.

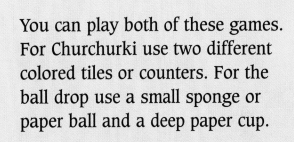

1. Which game is based on luck only?

2. Which game requires some skill? What are the possible outcomes for each game? Can you tell how likely each is before you play?

3. Which game do you like better? Explain.

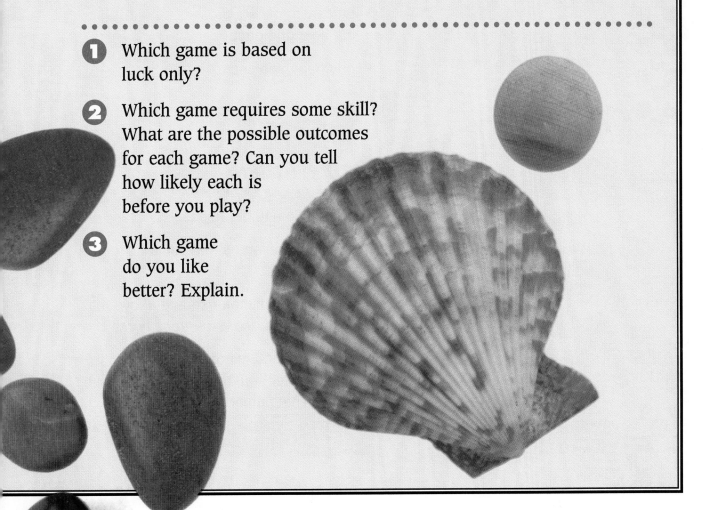

RACING SQUARES

Group

2 players

Materials

Each player needs:

- 2 number cubes

- 50 centimeter squares
  cut from grid paper

- grid paper labeled
  2 to 12

Game Rules:

1. Roll two number cubes.

2. Add the numbers that come up to get a sum.

3. Place a centimeter square above that sum on the grid paper race horse chart.

4. Keep going until one column of centimeter squares reaches the finish line. That number is the winner!

FINISH LINE

Each set of information below shows the results of an experiment. Study the information. Then copy and complete each drawing to show what the number cube, spinner, or bag of marbles might have looked like. Explain your reasoning.

1. 100 rolls of a number cube

outcome	number
1	54
2	31
3	15

2. 50 spins of a spinner

outcome	number
yellow	40
green	10

3. 500 rolls of a number cube

outcome	number
1	80
3	350
5	70

4. 100 spins of a spinner

outcome	number
blue	38
red	31
green	31

▶ For problems 5 and 6 the marble was replaced after each pick.

5. 200 picks from a bag with
5 marbles

outcome	number
red	80
blue	120

6. 300 picks from a bag with
6 marbles

outcome	number
black	203
red	47
green	50

Picking Pairs of Prizes

Large grab bag

Small grab bag

Raimundo

Wish List

Panda

yoyo

ON YOUR OWN

You pull a pair of jeans and a T-shirt out of your closet to wear. You have four colors of jeans: black, blue, red, and tan. You have four colors of T-shirts: black, white, blue, and green.

1. How many jean and T-Shirt combinations are possible?

Describe how likely you think it is that you will choose each of the following to wear.

2. a black or a green T-shirt

3. a pair of tan jeans

4. a pair of blue jeans and a white T-shirt

5. a pair of green jeans and a grey T-shirt

6. a pair of jeans

7. *My Journal:* What have you learned about solving combination problems? Explain.

What's The Combination?

▶ For each experiment 1 to 4:

a. Predict how likely the event is.

b. List all possible outcomes for the experiment.

c. Evaluate your prediction. How likely is the event?

d. Draw a line like the one below for each situation. Predict how likely the event is.

e. Write and describe your findings.

```
0          |          |          |          1
impossible  very     about      very      certain
           unlikely   even      likely
```

Experiment 1: toss a coin and spin the spinner at the right
Event: heads and green

Experiment 2: roll a number cube (1–6) and spin the spinner at the left
Event: even number and an A or a B

Experiment 3: choose two names from the bag, replace them, and draw again
Event: Albert and Rita

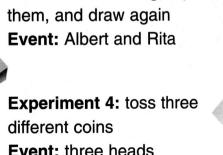

Experiment 4: toss three different coins
Event: three heads

1. Make up an outcome for spinning these two spinners which is very likely to occur. Write and tell why this is a very likely outcome.

 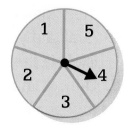

2. You and a friend each secretly choose one of the number cards below. How likely is it that you each choose the same number? If you each choose a number less than 30, how likely is it that you chose the same number?

43   52   38

27   66   71

3. Redraw the three spinners so that the chances of getting three yellows is very likely.

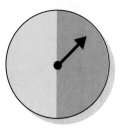 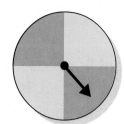 

4. *My Journal:* What have you learned about finding outcomes for combinations of two events?

Partners Again

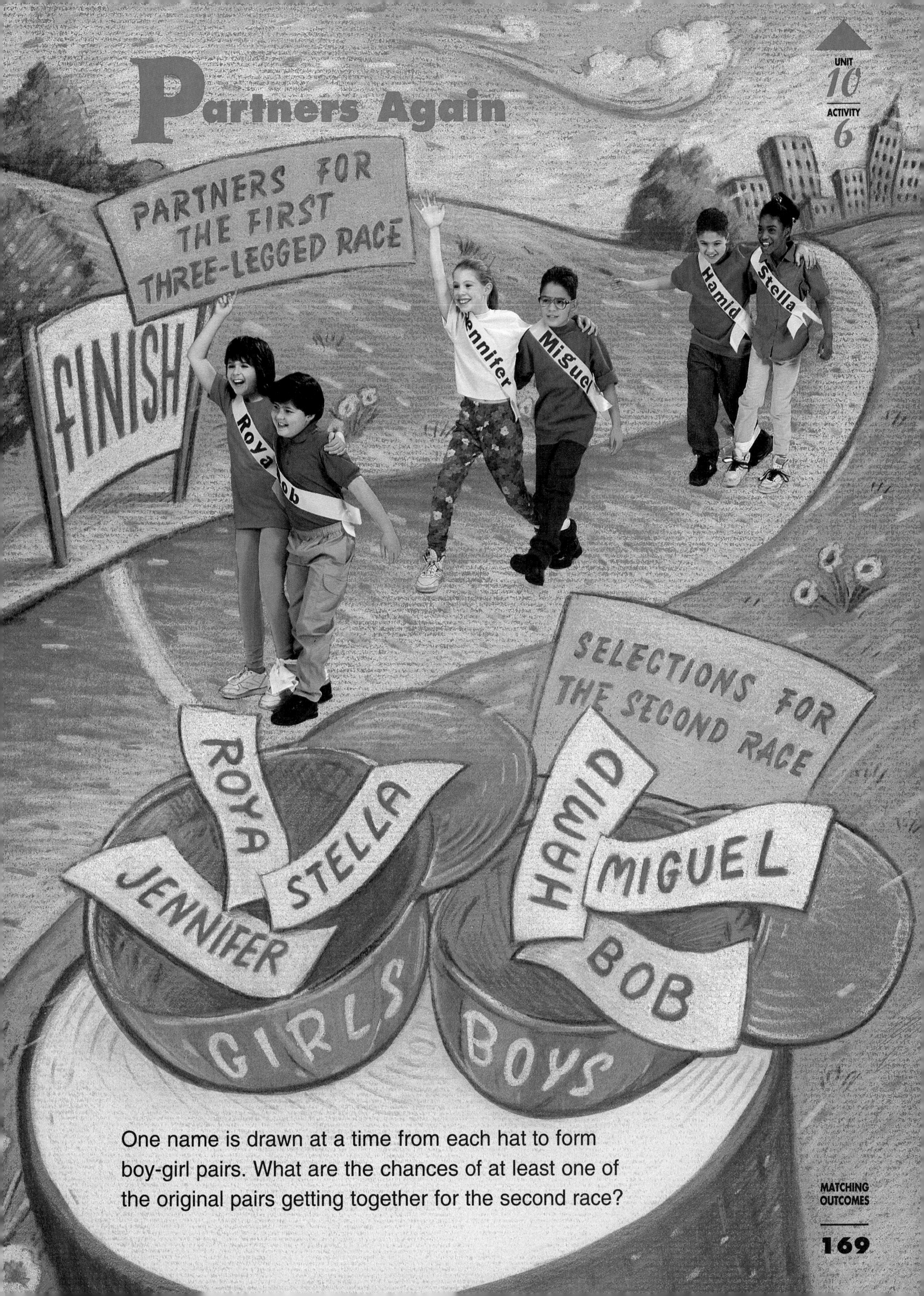

PARTNERS FOR THE FIRST THREE-LEGGED RACE
FINISH
Roya
Bob
Jennifer
Miguel
Hamid
Stella
SELECTIONS FOR THE SECOND RACE
ROYA
STELLA
JENNIFER
HAMID
MIGUEL
BOB
GIRLS
BOYS

One name is drawn at a time from each hat to form boy-girl pairs. What are the chances of at least one of the original pairs getting together for the second race?

WHAT ARE YOUR CHANCES?

Each box of a certain kind of cereal contains one of four different prizes. Suppose you went in a store and bought four boxes of this cereal. What are the chances that you will get all four prizes in these boxes?

One way is to use a spinner to do a simulation. Make a spinner like this one and use it to create a simulation of the prize problem.

Create a simulation
game to try to get
all four prizes. Make
a prediction before
you start. Play the
game to test
your prediction.

CheckYOURSELF

Great job! You created a simulation that matches the
conditions of the prize problem. You used the
simulation to help explain the chances of someone
getting 4 different prizes in 4 boxes.

$\mathcal{H}$ow can we describe motions?

Left, Right, Left, Right

ON YOUR OWN

Write and tell how slides and flips are used to make these designs.

1.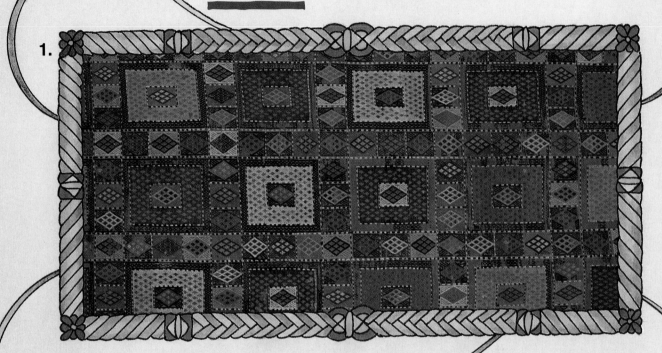

2.

3. *My Journal:* What did you learn that was new? Explain.

Flower Garden

ON
YOUR
OWN

▶ Tell how each figure was moved from the top position to the bottom.

1.

2.

3.

4.

5.

6.

Describe in writing how slides or flips were used in making these quilts.

7.

8.

9. *My Journal:* What have you learned about using slides and flips to make patterns? Explain.

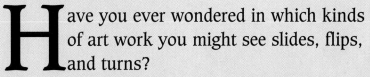

The Art of the Slides, Flips & Turns

PEOPLE, SOCIETY, AND MATHEMATICS

Have you ever wondered in which kinds of art work you might see slides, flips, and turns?

The ancient Indian art of floor painting, called rangoli , uses a mixture of flour, powdered lentils, turmeric and indigo, to create designs that include slides, flips and turns. This art which is practiced in Indian homes today honors both the home and the earth.

These intricate designs are made on the floor or doorstep in the morning and swept away at night with a grass broom indicating that it is the creation of the design and not the product that is important.

The Navajo of the Southwest United States use powdered colored rock to make sand or dry paintings for special ceremonies. They also were temporary and destroyed after the ceremonies.

1 Have you ever seen chalk drawings on a city sidewalk? How are these like rangoli? How do they differ?

2 Draw a simple object or design. Slide, flip, and turn it to make your own pattern. How would you use your pattern? Do you think it is more like Indian or Navajo art?

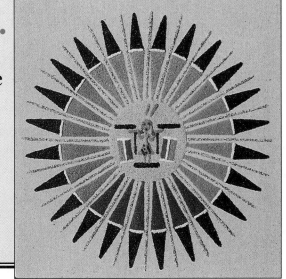

179

As the Flower Turns

TURNS—
USING
A POINT
ON THE
FIGURE

180

▶ Use the blocks:

1. Make a design that has turn symmetry of three.

2. Make a design that has turn symmetry of four.

Some animals have line symmetry; one half is a flip of the other half. Some animals have turn symmetry; if you rotate them a complete turn around a center point, they match themselves at least once during one complete rotation.

3. Which animals have line symmetry? Which have turn symmetry? Give reasons for your answers.

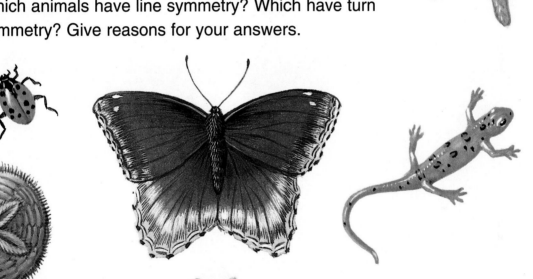

4. These blocks ⬡ ▲ have both line symmetry and turn symmetry. How many lines of symmetry does each shape have? How many times does it match itself during one complete turn or rotation?

5. *My Journal:* Which problem was the most interesting to you? Explain.

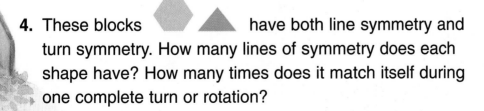

TURNS—
USING
A POINT
ON THE
FIGURE

181

... **T**urn, Turn, Turn

ON YOUR OWN

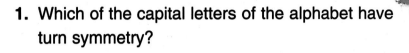

1. Which of the capital letters of the alphabet have turn symmetry?

2. Which have line symmetry?

3. How would your findings differ if you used small or lowercase letters?

4. Write a symmetric word.

5. What state has a line symmetric name?

6. *My Journal:* Did you find looking at line or turn symmetry easier? Explain.

COVERING the WALL

Make a wallpaper design that you would like to see in an entire room.

- Include examples of: slides, flips, turns, line symmetry and turn symmetry.

- Write to tell how you made your design and how you used all the motions.

CheckYOURSELF

Great job! Your wallpaper design shows examples of slides, flips, and turns. You identified all examples of line and turn symmetry. You explained clearly in writing how you made your design.

Acknowledgments

ILLUSTRATION

Cover Illustration: **Seymour Chwast**
Kevin Bapp: 40; **Christiane Beauregard:** 94, 174, 175; **Jennifer Bolten:** 56, 57, 150, 151; **Ken Bowser:** 73, 88, 89, 100, 101; **Neverne Covington:** 96-98; **Jerry Dadds:** 146, 147; **Mary DePalma:** 20, 21; **Regan Dunnick:** 2-4; **Matt Faulkner:** 77, 78, 115, 124, 125; **Tara Framer:** 118, 119; **Brad Gaber:** 26, 27, 126-130; **Kevin Hawkes:** 46, 47, 182, 183; **Obadinah Heavner:** 5, 6; **Jennifer Hewitson:** 50, 51,98; **Tom Huffman:** 113, 114; **Mark Kaplan:** 60, 61; **Salem Krieger:** 162-164; **Joe Lemonnier:** 37, 42, 50, 51, 52, 63, 72, 73, 78, 79, 84, 85, 88-91, 93, 124, 125, 132-134, 136-138, 162, 163; **Joe Lertola:** 29-31; **Keith E. Lo Bue:** 167; **Claude Martinot:** 93, 108, 109, 137-139; **Barbara Maslen:** 28; **Frank McShane:** 72, 79; **Marc Mongeau:** 16, 17; **Yu Cha Pak:** 90, 92; **Victoria Raymond:** 84; **Eric Rhinehart:** 63; **Michael Sours Rohani:** 74, 75, 169; **Robert Roper:** 52, 53, 110-112; **Dorothea Sierra:** 80, 81; **Kenneth Spengler:** 24, 25; **Russ Steffens** 86, 87; **Julia Talcott:** 156, 157; **Kat Thacker:** 106, 107; **Randy Verougstraete:** 54, 55; **Leslie Watkins:** 180, 181; **Vicki Wehrman:** 176-178.

PHOTOGRAPHY

Photo Management and Picture Research: **Omni-Photo Communications, Inc.**
Claire Aich: 12-15, 32-35, 46, 47, 85, 154, 155, 169-173, 184, 185; ©**American Hurrah, NYC:** 45; ©**Anderson/Monkmeyer Press:** 8, 9; ; ©**Art Resource:** 175; ©**Danilo Boschung/Leo De Wys:** 66,67; ©**Scott Camazine/Photo Researchers:** 141; **Country Floors:** 174; ©**Culver Pictures:** 38; ©**Dollarhide/Monkmeyer Press:** 149; **Everett Studios:** 48, 49, 64-67, 80-83, 120-123, 120,-123, 142-145, 152, 153; ©**Barrie Fanton/Omni-Photo Communications:** 66, 67, 80, 81; ©**FPG:** 8; ©**Robert Frerck/Odyssey/Chicago:** 141; ©**Neal Graham/Omni-Photo Communications:** 160; ©**The Granger Collection:** 76; ©**Grant/Monkmeyer Press:** 8; ©**Lowell Georgia/Photo Researchers:** 66; **Horizon:** 11, 116, 117; **Richard Hutchings:** i, 10, 11, 68, 70, 94, 119; ©**B. Paulson/Armstrong Roberts:** 184,185; ©**Richard Pasley/Stock Boston:** 34; ©**Joyce Photographics/Photo Researchers:** 71; ©**Manfred Kage/Peter Arnold, Inc.:** 135, 136; ©**Thomas Ives/The Stock Market:** 179; **Ken Karp:** 8, 22, 23, 135, 160, 161, 172, 173; **John Lei:** 1, 5, 18, 19, 21, 56, 59, 62, 68, 69, 87, 106, 118, 108, 150, 166; ©**Harvey Lloyd/The Stock Market:** 41; ©**Mike Mazzashi/Stock Boston:** 39; ©**Nawrocki/Nawrocki Stock Photos:** 116, 117; **Steven Oglivy:** 7, 36, 37, 120, 121, 140, 141, 158, 159; ©**Scala/Art Resource:** 175; ©**Rene Sheret/Tony Stone Worldwide:** 8,9; ©**Graiton M. Smith/The Image Bank:** 39; ©**Eric A. Soder/Tom Stack & Associates:** 18, 19; ©**Stock Boston:** 152, 153; ©**The Stock Market:** 59; ©**Superstock:** 59; ©**R. Thompson/Omni-Photo Communications:** 91; ©**Tzovaras/Art Resource:** 41; ©**Wanda Warming/The Image Bank:** 39; ©**Richard Weiss/Peter Arnold, Inc.:** 35; ©**Jim Wilson/NYT Picture:** 148.

CALCULATORS

T-I 108
T-I Math Explorer

MANIPULATIVES

Link-Its
Power Polygons